AF541365

Speaking (of)
widows

The Unseen and the Unheard

Editors

Namita Sethi

Vasiraju Rajyalakshmi

Tarun Sharma

Published by
Renu Kaul Verma
Vitasta Publishing Pvt Ltd
4348/4C, Ansari Road, Daryaganj
New Delhi - 110 002
info@vitastapublishing.com

ISBN: 978-81-19670-52-9

First Edition 2025
MRP ₹595

Edited by Soham Debsarkar and Reena Singh
Layout & Cover Design by Rohit Gautam
Printed at Chaman Enterprises, New Delhi

*Dedicated to the Late Dr V Mohini Giri,
who fought relentlessly to give a
voice to widows*

Contents

Message From

Dr Meera Khanna

Trustee and President
Guild of Service

MOST OF US know of a widow and widowhood within our own families, communities, and extended families. But most of us are also unaware of the unique vulnerabilities widows face in our society; social isolation, cultural stigmatisation and economic dependency. Thus, this study has a unique significance as it has been conducted by young adults who set out on a journey of discovery of a community that rarely figures in poverty discourses or policy narratives.

Widowhood is not just a personal loss; it is often a gateway to social and economic marginalisation. Widows lose more than a spouse. That is the harsh reality in most patriarchal societies. Across the globe, widows often face profound challenges—social exclusion, economic deprivation, and a loss of status and support. These women encounter further hardships, driven by cultural norms and legal systems that deny them basic rights and opportunities.

Mahatma Gandhi said, 'The true measure of any society can be found in how it treats its most vulnerable members.' Widows, among the most vulnerable, deserve the attention and action of lawmakers, government, judiciary, civil society and communities. Yet, in many parts of the world, their struggles go unnoticed, and their voices remain unheard.

Through their research and interaction with the widows of Vrindavan, the students of Janki Devi College learnt that the challenges widows face are not just personal, but also deeply rooted in cultural norms and legal barriers that perpetuate their sufferings, and a system that subsumes their layered vulnerabilities within the homogenous community of women. What is even more encouraging for a women's rights activist like me is the sensitivity the students exhibited, the perception to see beyond the obvious, an understanding that empowering widows is not just a moral obligation; it is an essential step toward achieving gender equality and sustainable development and that widows are resilient within their personal struggles.

This study does indicate that if the right and timely support is given, widows can overcome these challenges and lead empowered lives, contributing to their families and communities. It might seem an almost impossible task. But as Nelson Mandela once said, 'It always seems impossible until it's done.'

I must congratulate Prof Swati Paul for her sensitised insights in supporting this unique study by the JDM College Centre For Gender Equity Studies Project. The study was guided by the very able leadership and excellent guidance of faculty members Namita Sethi, Vasiraju Rajyalakshmi and Tarun Sharma. Finally, my deep appreciation of the students who implemented the study with so much grace and perception. The collaboration between the college and the Guild for Service has been seamless, and appreciation is due to both institutions.

I hope that the study gets widely disseminated and paves the way for many more impactful collaborations between colleges and civil society organisations in the future.

Acknowledgements

THIS PROJECT COULD not have been possible without the active encouragement and support of Prof Swati Pal, Principal, Janki Devi Memorial College, and our collaborators, the Guild of Service, a national voluntary developmental organisation in consultative status with the Economic and Social Council (ECOSOC) of the United Nations, dedicated to the empowerment of marginalised women and children.

In this journey, we were constantly guided and inspired by the pioneering work of Dr Mohini Giri, to whom this book is lovingly dedicated.

We are deeply grateful to our resource persons Ms Meera Khanna, President, Guild of Service and the co-founder of Everywoman Treaty for Ending Violence against Women and Girls and Prof Malashri Lal. Both shared their knowledge, expertise, experience and time generously with the faculty and students of JDM College. Praise is also due to Ms Nivedita Das, member-in-charge, at Vrindavan, family therapist and gerontologist, and to Mr Manjit Singh for facilitating our team's visit to Ma Dham.

We owe a debt of gratitude to Prof Anita Singh of BHU for writing a Foreword, and to Prof Swati Pal for contributing an Afterword to this volume, so readily and graciously. We really appreciate the gift of your time.

Thank you also to the numerous 'Maas' we met, who shared their life stories, their hopes and fears with us, and who smiled for our students despite untold past trauma.

The students, led by Muskaan Jain and Arshpreet, displayed a refreshing enthusiasm for this research project and dedication to the larger cause. The editing and design of the students' research section were facilitated by Himanshi Chawla, Ananya, and the members of Lumiere, the photography society of JDMC. Thanks also to Samriddhi Pendharkar, Priya Khandelwal, Diksha, Sakshi Mishra, Niyati, Himanshi, Smriti Ahuja, Aanchal, and a host of other students who comprised the student team.

We are grateful to the faculty members whose contributions have lent academic rigour and a range of perspectives to the book. The office staff of JDMC, especially Mr Surendra Kumar, and Mr Arvind Pal, and the accounts department, especially Ms Pushpa Rawat and Mr Manpreet have been of immense help.

The book would not have taken shape without the endless hours of discussion, brainstorming, and teamwork by the three editors Namita, Rajyalakshmi and Tarun with each other and with the numerous scholars they interacted with.

Last, but not least, thank you to Ms Renu Kaul Verma of Vitasta.

Foreword

Professor Anita Singh
Department of English,
BHU, Varanasi

'GOD WILLING, SHE'LL be reborn as a man,' observed an older widow named Bhagavati, about the nine-year-old widow Chuiya in the 2005 film *Water*. The film delves into the practice of isolating widows and enforcing lifelong chastity and the renouncement of material yearnings, highlighting long-standing concerns surrounding the status of widows. Widowhood requires the formation of new relationships within families, kinship groups, and communities. When such relationships prove difficult, many widows seek refuge in charitable institutions known as ashrams, facing significant social, economic, and cultural challenges. Historically, there have been three primary approaches to addressing the widow issue in India: the practice of widow immolation (Sati), relegating older and non-reproductive widows to menial household roles, and relocating them to distant spiritual sites such as Vrindavan, Mathura, or Varanasi. In her 1998 work, *Contentious Traditions,* Lata Mani examines the colonial debate on Sati against the backdrop of the civilising missions of colonialism. She highlights how this debate reveals a complex interplay of interests, often obscuring the experiences and subjectivity of the widows themselves.

Within nationalist discourses, women's roles in relation to the nation and the national family often inhabits an idealised or fantastical realm. For centuries, the national imagination invoked traditional ideals of motherhood, promoting domesticity and sexual control, framing women as wives, mothers, and goddesses, and depicting 'India as mother' and as a cultural motif that shaped the gendered politics of the emerging nation. In this context, widows became symbols of the national narrative, largely defined by their self-imposed sexual restraint. The marginalisation of widows and their removal to holy places like Vrindavan, Varanasi or Mathura likely stemmed from societal expectations of self-sacrificing womanhood and the inability of families to integrate widows into traditional family structures. It is estimated that there are over 40 million widows in India, many of whom experience a life similar to a 'living sati,' a reference to the now-banned practice of widow burning. In Vrindavan or Varanasi, widows are dispersed, with some residing in government institutions, others in private homes, and many living in groups.

In the twenty-first century, widowed women encounter a range of troubling issues beyond the emotional distress of losing their spouse. These challenges include, but are not limited to, social exclusion, loss of income, and even loss of housing. Additionally, problems related to widow remarriage, dowry, and sati persist, further complicating their situation. In 2024, the National Human Rights Commission (NHRC) of India issued an advisory highlighting ten key areas for action. This advisory urges Central and State Government authorities, as well as Union Territory administrations, to enhance efforts in safeguarding the welfare of widows and protecting their human rights.

The significance of this book draws on the examination of the complexities surrounding widowhood in India. This work was accomplished by the Gender Equity Studies Centre of Janki Devi Memorial College collaborating with the Guild of Service to investigate the challenges faced by widows, particularly in the northern parts of India. The first section of the book explores both the socio-economic challenges and systemic discrimination faced by widows, and examines governmental initiatives aimed at addressing these issues.

The second section explores how the literary representation of widows—through characters from epics such as in the Mahabharata and an examination of Indira Goswami's experiences—serves as a means of encouraging empathy and engagement from readers. The fundamental aim of using an interplay of geography, mythology, and the lived realities of widows is criticism and correction of culture.

The sociological analyses in the third section deepen the discussion by contrasting the status of widows with society's focus on marriage. The research provides a contemporary viewpoint by highlighting community efforts to empower widows.

In its fourth section, the book wraps up with student-conducted fieldwork, capturing the real experiences of widows in Vrindavan. This hands-on approach adds depth to the academic discourse, incorporating interviews and observations that bring a personal touch to the statistical data.

I am immensely pleased to write the foreword for *Speaking (of) Widows.* I appreciate the sincere efforts of the editors Namita Sethi, Vasiraju Rajyalakshmi and Tarun Sharma and the Principal, Prof Swati Pal in bringing together this insightful and substantial volume and providing new perspectives and a broader context for understanding the far-reaching impact of gender parity as it explores the multifaceted experiences of widows, examining theoretical frameworks, literary depictions, and sociological studies.

Taken as a whole, the book offers a substantial contribution to the discussion on widowhood in India, blending academic research with empathetic narratives. It encourages readers to scrutinise societal norms and reflect on the broader impact of widows' voices, advocating for greater understanding and proactive measures.

(Prof Anita Singh teaches English at Banaras Hindu University in UP, India)

Introduction

Namita Sethi

Setting the Context

WIDOWHOOD IS NOT a curse or a blighted condition of life; it is a natural stage in the cycle of life, and is the same, culturally, for men and women. And yet, it comes attached with a cluster of assumptions, stereotypes, taboos, rituals, tragic circumstances, and discrimination for both real and imagined women. In a culture as heterogenous as that of India, it is very challenging to map the continuities and discontinuities with older representations of widows. Nevertheless, it is crucial to chart the evolution of ideas about widows and register these changes in literary, as well as popular culture representations. A study of cultural constructions supplements changes at the level of policy and practices for empowering widows. It continues to be relevant even today.

According to 2020 statistics, there are around 55 million widows in India, and quite a few among the elderly are likely to be widowed. In 2015, more than 80 per cent of the population over the age of seventy constituted widows. A third of all widows worldwide, live in India and China, with India overtaking China

(44.6 million) to become the country with the largest number of widows. The COVID-19 pandemic also caused a drastic increase in the number of widows. Furthermore, the incidence of violence against women and abuse is well-known among widows of all ages. How far do we register the presence of this large number of widows in our country?

Widows have often been depicted as the forgotten women, as observed in the title of the film *The Forgotten Woman* (2008), directed by Dileep Mehta and written by Deepa Mehta, for their erasure from the collective mindset. Sadly, a vast majority continue to struggle for survival, invisible to the state, and even when economically better off, are expected to live colourless lives. The white clothes prescribed for the widows by tradition carry the symbolism of abstinence, self-deprivation, and sacrifice that are not discarded, even when they resume wearing coloured attire. This study draws upon disciplines such as literature, history, sociology, law, and policy to generate a report based on fieldwork and an overview of cultural perceptions and transitions.

This faculty-student project began with a few questions: Are the state and society, with their correctional mechanisms, laws and policies paying adequate attention to this issue? Have the popular perceptions about, and cultural representations of widowhood in India changed with time? In what ways is a woman's experience of losing a life partner different from that of a man? What brings widows to holy cities like Vrindavan and Varanasi?

The word *vidhwa* derives from the Sanskrit root *vidh,* which signifies destitution. Many Indian widows flock to the holy cities of Varanasi (Kashi in ancient times, Benares in the colonial era), Vrindavan, and Mathura for various reasons that have been explored in the essays in this volume. Vrindavan was chosen over Varanasi as the specific site of our research due to its proximity to

Delhi and the ease of access for the college research team.

As a counterpoint to the examples from literature, sociology, popular culture and policy making in the essays, the students' research provides an anecdotal entry point, and is based on fieldwork and interviews with the widows of Vrindavan, and also the popular viewpoints about widows today. We hope that this dual lens sheds light on what more needs to be done by the state and society to ensure equal opportunities and humane conditions for widows. Awareness will generate better practices at the level of the state as well as sensitivity on the part of the family and society. It is also an attempt to bring the widow back into the discourse and to look at more recent representations.

The challenges as well as the empowering strategies for widows should not be subsumed into the larger rubric of Women's Studies, to the point of erasure. The physical and mental health challenges faced by them also form a special area of our enquiry. We wanted to provide solid research about ground reality and policies that are helpful to widows by bringing together academics and activism together with fieldwork and data.

For this research, the Gender Equity Studies Centre of the Janki Devi Memorial College joined hands with the Guild of Service, to study the challenges faced by widows in India, especially in the northern belt, and give suggestions for better policy formation, implementation and best practice suggestions. The project began with raising awareness among college students towards the plight of widows followed by an interaction with them at Vrindavan.

The Team

Janki Devi Memorial College (JDMC) was founded in 1959, by Brij Krishan Chandiwala and was named after his mother. He belonged to a flourishing family of silver merchants, and despite hailing from a trading background, fervently believed in the cause of women's education, especially for those less privileged, as well as for women from business families, who were usually denied higher education. JDMC has a long-standing history of empowering young women, raising awareness about gender-related issues, encouraging research in areas that fall under Women's Studies and promoting social outreach programmes. It was thc first college to set up a Gender Studies Resource Centre, outside the main university campus which saw the establishment of the Women's Studies and Development Centre (WSDC) in 1987. The college has been working with the WSDC actively for decades.

The Centre for Gender Equity Studies identified the plight of widows in India as a topic for special investigation for 2022-2023. The students were led by three faculty members of JDMC: Namita Sethi, Vasiraju Rajyalakshmi and Tarun Sharma. The student constitution was multi-disciplinary at the college level, inviting participation from all departments within the college.

The field visit was facilitated by the Guild of Service, New Delhi, an NGO in consultative status with ECOSOC, United Nations. It is dedicated to the empowerment of marginalised women and children and has an exemplary field record in the area of widow support. In fact, one of the objectives was to examine Ma Dham (run by the Guild) as a case study of good practices in giving homeless widows a sanctuary and a meaningful life by providing them with many avenues.

Methodology

For the survey, we included widows who avail state/centre benefits to assess the benefits of the current schemes and policies, as well as homeless widows living in shelters and even street widows. The questionnaires examined the changes in these women's social lives, both pre and post-widowhood. Semi-structured, face-to-face interviews were conducted with lawyers, and stakeholders, including, but not limited to, NGOs, people found on the streets of Vrindavan, college students, and widows across sites. There were also questionnaires circulated in Delhi to find out about the younger generation's perceptions of widows in their circle. The primary data was drawn from questionnaires and case studies based on interviews. The questionnaire survey followed random sampling, and students were trained to be sensitive, empathetic and to some extent, intuitive in receiving answers.

The students held brainstorming sessions in which they discussed the findings of their pre-visit surveys. They were given reading materials and access to documentaries and films to acquaint themselves with the status of widows and the beliefs surrounding them in the Indian subcontinent. During the field visits, they were encouraged to move beyond a theoretical understanding of this issue by speaking to both street widows and widows living in government-run shelters to contextualise their socio-economic status along with commonly held religious and traditional beliefs. Lawyers, writers, artists and activists were invited to share their experiences at workshops and two national seminars that were organised in the college.

We are grateful for the interaction with the Guild of Service for the help offered to study the ground situation at Vrindavan, and identify the challenges that need to be addressed with changes in law, policy and practice.

Discussions focussed on the legal rights of widows, facilitating claims to natal inheritance by women/widows and relationship/dating/re-marriage for both widows and widowers.

The overall aim was to contemporise a topic that is usually found at the margins of gender studies and attempt to bring together fiction, activism, law and policy, as well as changes in social perceptions over the years. Special attention was paid to accounts relating to the inaccessibility of state support and the extent of economic support from families, to help formulate the best practices to help widows live a life of dignity.

Some Findings Based on the Vrindavan Visit

The amount doled out to widows across different states is varied and contingent upon changing political fortunes to an extent. We suggest that schemes supporting widows should be changed into a fixed, uniform policy, done through an Act. The amount must match current inflation rates.

Work/films on this topic have focused primarily on abandoned Bengal widows. The profile of widows flocking to religious sites like Vrindavan has changed considerably in recent years. A vast majority of the widows in Uttar Pradesh are now coming there because they cannot adjust with their sons and daughters-in-law. These changing trends should be documented.

Data related to mental health challenges and health support, in general, needs to be collected. How can the state support the physical and mental health, especially of elderly resourceless widows, for whom even travelling to a hospital is challenging.

Along with policy changes and effective implementation, mindsets and cultural perceptions about widowhood must change. This state is a sad event, not a disability.

Government and lawmaking bodies try to do their bit to ameliorate the lot of homeless women including daughters and widows, but it is grossly inadequate. The abuse, neglect and discrimination, sometimes intense trauma that widows in India undergo, needs immediate attention from policy makers.

Even when housed in the comfort of protective environs like a committed NGO, past trauma results in immense physical and mental health concerns for widows.

Abandoned or forgotten by their families, friends, and support circles, these women take recourse to living a life of obscurity in retreats sanctioned by religious traditions, but not all are able to live a life of dignity. More needs to be done by all of us than just salvaging our conscience by donating money for their shelters.

This Book

This book charts the journey between speaking of widows and speaking widows.

Section I has an essay by famous author and activist, Meera Khanna, President of the Guild of Service, who theorises the need to focus on widows to alleviate poverty. She draws on years of experience to suggest positive reforms in law and policy. Samriddhi's essay also lists and assesses the initiatives taken by the Indian Government to address the needs of widows.

The second section looks at texts and literary contexts. Widows have been silenced and talked about rather than being given a voice. The word 'of' has, therefore, been put in parenthesis so that is able to hear that voice.

Were representations of widowhood always regressive and centred around the axis of victimhood? Taking a close look at the epics can reveal some very powerful and influential women, who were widows, for example, Satyavati and Kunti in the Mahabharata.

We attempted to study the evolution of the discursive category of *vaidhavya* or widowhood from ancient Indian literature to contemporary writings in Indian languages. Apart from abandoned and abused widows usually found at pilgrimage sites, the book examines other kinds of representations of empowerment as well as of regulation of sexuality and socio-economic challenges faced by widows, as narrated by themselves or as represented in texts and popular culture.

Prof Malashri Lal's essay draws upon her association with Indira Goswami to examine *Neel Kanthi Braja* (1982), which can be read as a veiled autobiography of Goswami. It is based on Goswami's experiences with the Radhaswamy sect of Vrindavan widows, whom she lived with upon becoming a widow. Lal's essay fuses the geography of Braja and the mythology of Radha and Krishna to engage with the duality of the Vrindavan of our imagination and the lived reality of the widows' experiences there, as explored in fiction and other writing.

Namita Sethi examines post-Independence and contemporary fiction's imaging of widows. She links these representations to the injunctions laid upon widows, while also tracing resistance and empowerment, in both classical Indian literature and the period of colonial reform, including the pioneering efforts of Ishwar Chandra Vidyasagar.

Ankan Dhar offers a perspective on the Hindu widow in colonial Bengal. He looks at the work of Sarat Chandra Chattopadhyay in the context of the Widow Remarriage Act of 1856 and the Age of Consent debates of 1890-92. His study locates the appropriation, and the reformulation of the figure of the widow within the larger rubric of national identity formation.

Ruchika Bhatia explores images of widows in contemporary advertisements. She observes the neglect of a whole category of consumers, thought to be unimportant, and asserts the need for more positive and empowering representations in the media.

Section III offers a more sociological perspective. Prof Rajyalakshmi writes on the status of widows by looking at its binary opposite: the immense importance given to marriage in an Indian woman's life. She emphasises the importance of empowering widows and safeguarding their rights and suggests ways to achieve these outcomes.

Vandana Madan bases her observations on her three-decade-long association with Vrindavan and its widows. She speculates about facets of the widows' 'forced renunciation' and its cultural, as well as spiritual repercussions. She reads it as an act of rebellion against an unjust society, and of transcendence at once.

Tarun Sharma's research was conducted at Lado Sarai, an urban village in South Delhi. He examines the treatment of widows by society and offers examples of empowerment and support offered by the village community to widows, thus offering an alternative social model.

Section IV registers the impressions and the results of surveys conducted by students at different locations in Vrindavan. The students followed the lives of widows across streets and ghats, outside temples and on Parikrama Marg. They entered Bhajan Ashrams and shelters for widows, and spent time at Ma Dham, the visit facilitated by the Guild. There are overviews about government policies, as well as candid interviews with widows they met in temples, markets and on the roads leading up to tourist and pilgrimage spots. They also conducted surveys among college students prior to their field visit and upon their return. The pictures they took tell their own story.

Observations from Ma Dham Shelter

The Ma Dham office is meticulous about maintaining records, right from the date of arrival of each Ma, to preserving their identity card and other documents, often helping them apply for and source these for the more senior Mas, who find themselves in an extremely vulnerable situation without government documentation. The women, more often than not, no longer have access to their own ration cards, Aadhaar cards, bank accounts, and property papers, and this makes them invisible to state agencies. The staff at the shelter works hard to get them this access, a difficult task, as the documents required for the process have cither been left behind by the widows at their hometowns, or they were never made in the first place. We are grateful to Ms Kajal, the counsellor at the office for sharing the records of the widows. We picked a few at random, and then proceeded to interview them. To protect the identity of the subjects, only their initials have been mentioned. The investigation questions included the following:

1. Age and social background of the widow.
2. Date of arrival in Vrindavan and the date of arrival at the Ma Dham shelter.
3. Reason for arrival and stay: whether religious, caste or class-based, whether under duress, abandoned or any other.
4. Whether they got a share in property.
5. Reason for being denied property rights.
    a. No title deed/documentation
    b. Papers were taken away
    c. Property given away to children or family members
    d. Ill-treatment by in-laws
    e. Whether her parents or brother denied her a share in property
    f. Lack of awareness
6. Incidence of assault or unwanted sexual overtures.
7. Whether they enjoy devotional singing/chanting.
8. Whether they are compensated for singing *bhajans* (Ma

Dham discourages begging or dependence).
9. What changes would they like to see in society.
10. Whether they wear coloured attire?

Some Responses

MD (caste unknown) arrived in 2014, at the age of 70, from Bihar, five years after the demise of her husband. She has a walking disability. There was no one at her home to take care of her special needs or help her with mobility. She came because she felt helpless and needed support. She has no share in the family (marital) property. MD left her marital home because she was treated poorly and did not receive anything from her parental home, either. She enjoys devotional singing and does not expect any compensation. She does not wish anyone else to go through what she did. In that, she would definitely want to see change.

PB arrived from Bengal and is a Kayastha. She has been here since 2010, and is now 94. The other shelters were reluctant to take her in because she was quite advanced in age and was not in good health. She came of her own volition. Widowed at an early age, she has a son and all her property papers were taken away from her. The son had the property transferred in his name after forcibly taking her signature. She sings bhajans voluntarily. She would like to see a change in traditions and family structure in West Bengal, from where she hails. She used to wear only white, but now wears coloured saris.

PA, from Uttar Pradesh is from the Agarwal caste, and has been here since 2014 and is now 60 years old. She had mental health issues since childhood and was abandoned in Vrindavan by her *devar* (husband's younger brother) after her husband passed away. The brother-in-law usurped her property and money—she used the term, '*hadap liye*'. She was deeply distressed as she used to tie her brother-in-law, a *rakhi* and considered him her brother, but he betrayed her by abandoning her in Vrindavan, where she knew no one. He also forcibly took away all her papers and documents.

She enjoys devotional singing and even dancing but does this only within the Ma Dham premises. She is overwrought, and at times, hysterical, but very aware of the trauma that the family betrayal caused her.

RDS, a Bengali Brahmin, arrived in Vrindavan at age 56. She had mental health issues. Her husband left her and remarried, so technically, she is not a widow. In an interesting twist, the second wife was willing to 'adjust' and was content to be a co-wife, but RDS stood her ground and refused to accept bigamy. She says she prefers staying at the shelter to staying in her marital home. She neither got share in the property or alimony. She voluntarily adopted the status of a widow after leaving her marital home in disgust. While she has renounced and disowned her husband, without a formal divorce, she still observes the *karvachauth* fast to ensure his long life and well-being. The second wife observes this fast, as well. RDS seems to have been abandoned by her birth family as well. She likes bhajans and wearing coloured clothes. She would like better support for mental health issues and looks forward to a change in the societal mindset towards those facing mental health challenges.

PS from Chhattisgarh is of the OBC caste and came to the Ma Dham Ashram in 2017 at the age of 70. She has spine issues which makes it difficult for her to walk erect. She came of her own volition because of her disability, poverty and need for support. She has no surviving family members. She had to sell her 50 *gaz* land to pay for her husband's treatment during his terminal illness. She got no share in property from her brother or parents. She does not like *bhajans* and thinks of singing as 'noise' and cannot bear it. She would like to see a scheme for universal education for girls being implemented and more avenues for women's employment. She learnt to read and write late in life and would like all women to have access to literacy and education. She prefers coloured garments.

Kiran Dasi is 108 years old and has lived at Ma Dham since 1988. She has a daughter and grandchildren. Apparently, she earned her living by begging on the streets, which her family disapproved of. The records observe that her temperament was very domineering when she arrived. The family seemed accepting of her overall, but perhaps a need for independence drove her to seek shelter at the ashram. Property was not an issue in this case according to records of a previous interview. She likes being at Ma Dham, and the shelter is justifiably proud of housing her. She is often regarded as a mascot for the success of this model home.

GP, a Bengali Kayastha widow arrived here in 2009. She is reticent and reluctant to reveal details of her life and speaks only in Bangla. She cited spiritual and religious reasons for coming to Vrindavan and said that coming to Kashi (Varanasi), Mathura or Vrindavan, and leading an ascetic life of a widow shall ensure she does not attract widowhood in her next birth. She got no share in either her natal or marital property. She says this is because widows are treated in a certain way in Bengal, and are not expected to demand a share. Once she was widowed, she was treated badly by her in-laws and was indifferent to the topic of social change. It is likely that her 'couldn't care less' attitude is a kind of post-traumatic stress disorder, according to her counsellor.

SB, a Bengali Brahmin widow came to the shelter seeking peace of mind. Whether her lack of desire for anything in life is borne of genuine spiritual detachment or is based on what she thinks people expect her to say, is hard to determine. She is generous with the free gifts and *daan* that comes her way as a Vrindavan widow, and distributes them to her family regularly. Though young, she does not want to remarry or have children. She claims she has seen far too many tragic tales of wives and mothers and ill-treatment by family members. She counsels women to adopt rather than give birth. In her case, the effect of trauma as well as conditioning needs to be further explored.

Observations about Opportunities and Challenges

Based upon these and other interviews, as well as the interactions with the women in a large group, and with the management, certain interesting facts emerged:

- The staff at Ma Dham help the Mas to get an Aadhaar card, which is an essential identity document required for registration, voting, travel, banking, claiming pension, skill education, employment and just about everything needed to survive in India today. The first step in their rehabilitation proves the toughest. Since most of these women are old and not educated, they cannot always sign their names, and getting their biometric identification proves challenging as their thumbprints are not easy to obtain and identify consistently. Most of them have poor eyesight as well. The government does not provide funding for getting the Aadhaar made, which at last count, costs a minimum of Rs 130 per person.
- The paperwork needed to get these women access to their late husband's pension takes a minimum of one and a half years. For opening a bank account, an identity document and ration card are needed, which is not always easy to come by.
- A PAN card is needed for each of them. Documentation is essential for pension as well as getting government benefits under low-income group and other schemes.

- To open a bank account, one needs an income certificate, for which zero balance accounts are made at Jan Soochna Kendra. Since, the widows' access to digitisation and technology is severely limited, the shelter's intervention is essential. All these steps are needed to show and prove that the widows need the aid and money. Only then can they be registered under any scheme at all. Most of them experience the independence of owning and operating a bank account for the first time in their lives.
- Pension Card: For this, the husband's death certificate is needed, which is often not easily obtained. Sometimes, the widows genuinely do not have access to the paperwork, and at other times, they cannot be bothered to follow up as they are bewildered by the unending rules and need for documentation. They sometimes cannot comprehend the importance of documentation because of lack of awareness.
- Most of the widows that arrive at Ma Dham come there after being rejected at other shelters because they need special attention either because of their advanced age, need for medical assistance and support, need for mental health support and counselling, a sustained regimen of treatment and expensive drugs, doctor visits, and disability support.
- A lot of the issues that widows face intersect with geriatric care and mental health support which need to be factored in by the government, support agencies, and policymakers before identifying their requirements accurately. For example, Meera Khanna of Guild of Service suggested that more than endless donations of sweets and blankets, the widows need more unglamourous and basic provisions like adult diapers, psychiatric and arthritic drugs that are fairly expensive. Even transportation costs to a good hospital, such as to the mental

hospital in Agra can be very high. Patience and sensitivity is needed to liaise with doctors, lawyers and government agencies on behalf of the Mas.

- About the safety and prevention of exploitation of widows, mainly the younger ones, not much data could be obtained. The ones at Ma Dham seem protected and did not experience assault or abuse. However, this is an issue that is usually brushed under the carpet in Vrindavan, which is a holy city. Interviewees were very reluctant to talk on the subject. More studies need to be done to ascertain the experience of street widows and single women in the city, in this regard.
- The average profile of those seeking shelter at Ma Dham and other shelter options is that of mature and older women. From what could be inferred from interviews with widows outside of Ma Dham, younger women prefer squatting on the streets or renting a room at Rs1,000 a month. Squatting on the streets helps them earn approximately Rs 400 per day along with an additional income of Rs 300 that they can make from bhajan-singing at ashrams. In addition, they get some rations and can also sell the excess rations and other material that are donated to them. The widows at the shelter are, however, discouraged from indulging in such activities, though they regularly head out for *baata-baati* and for big donation drives at temples.
- There is no restriction on the mobility of widows at Ma Dham, unlike at some other government shelters where they feel great constraint.

In the past, the majority of the widows were from Bengal and eastern India, because of the common social bias against widows in these areas. Widows' entitlement to property is widely recognised and most often, spurs greed on the part of the family members who want to deprive them of their entitlement.

However, a change has been perceived in recent years by the staff at Ma Dham. In addition to UP, a lot of women are also coming from nearby states like Haryana, Rajasthan, Delhi, and Bihar to escape ill-treatment at the hands of their families. Some cases include mothers-in-law who have differences with their daughters-in-law. Ironically, they seldom blame the son, even if it is the son who deprives them of their share in property. Some are reluctant to speak of their family in public altogether, which stems perhaps from them not wanting to shame their own family.

Avenues and Opportunities

Those interviewed expressed satisfaction with the green and open surroundings at the Ma Dham, and the ability to mentor children on the premises if desired. Some love the cows and calves at the in-house *gau shala*, while others find spiritual succour in the multi-faith prayer rooms on the campus. Some have volunteered to train for skill enhancement that the shelter offers and have even become successful entrepreneurs. One of the strengths of Ma Dham is the networking between various agencies. During our visit, we saw the Mas make little gift bags from recycled material for packaging organic seeds to be given as gifts for organic farming to nearby villages, in association with the NGO, Nav Danya.

The Mas also learn about and contribute to sustainability and ecology. Vegetables, fruits and flowers bloom in the gardens, where residents often volunteer. They appreciate and participate in the cultural programmes, festivities, and talks that are regularly organised for them. The widows at Ma Dham love to talk to visitors and were especially curious about the DU college girls who had come to meet them. They were spontaneous and happy to answer their questions. This was refreshing because often, the widows who have become adept at answering questions posed by the media and researchers who throng to Vrindavan can make up the answers they think the questioner wants to hear. They even invent facts about their background and experience to reiterate a certain perception or pre-conceived notions. The students were duly alerted and sensitised to this possibility before they began their research. On the whole, their youth, and open and enthusiastic demeanour may have elicited more candid responses from the widows. The primary school on the premises, which provides quality education to underprivileged children from nearby areas provides another model of supporting the local economy and promoting an integrative approach to development. At the emotional level, the presence of happy, beaming, friendly and curious children considerably uplifted the spirits of our volunteers as well as of the ashram staff and residents. The enthusiasm of the children is infectious and radiates positivity, marking Ma Dham distinct from some of the more gloomier places that the team also visited at Vrindavan.

The inter-generational aspect of the interaction helped us glean the big strength of the Ma Dham model.

Challenges

The biggest challenge was the mental health issues and senility that seems to affect some of the resident widows. On the one hand, the Dham provides them emotional and physical support, clean hygienic meals with a varied menu, and safe and comfortable housing; on the other hand, some of the widows have been dehumanised by past traumas. When they come here, they are already riddled with behavioural issues, and because there is a lack of recognition and support for mental health patients in small towns in India, these abandoned women have nowhere else to go. Some of the women have personality disorders like narcissism and borderline schizophrenia, which necessitate proper evaluation and ongoing support.

As in any group housing and old age homes, fights are common among residents. These are usually petty such as fighting over a bucket and mug in the washroom, and are handled patiently by the staff but sometimes minor incidents of violence can take place. Occasionally, the widows display apathy if a resident passes away, with only the roommate responding with an expression of grief. As a trauma response, some of the widows can seem to be manipulative and devoid of emotion. The shelter does its best to give these women a degree of space, but often, a single unit has to accommodate up to four women. Although, each woman has a separate bed, sharing the space with others brings its own challenges. The street widows, in contrast, choose to constantly brave danger to preserve a degree of independence, rather than be part of a government shelter.

Implications for Policy and Good Practices

- Despite all these measures, there is an urgent need to address the issues of the widows' housing and support on the part of policymakers. The sum allocated for their pension under various schemes is highly inadequate keeping in mind the inflation, and their special needs that include disability, mental health and geriatric care. The sum varies across cities and states and needs to be re-evaluated realistically, based on the latest research.
- The needs of the younger, educated, and more independent widows should be dealt with differently from those who are

completely dependent on shelters and the state. The latter are mostly women either abandoned by their families or have left their families for various distressing reasons, not necessarily religious or spiritual.

- The government and administration must make special provisions to ensure them easier access to their identity documents, PAN cards, bank accounts and other paperwork, along with free legal and medical services.

Perceptions

The profiling is still ambiguous. Often married women who are unhappy in their marriages, and wish to avoid the social stigma of divorce and separation, embrace the identity of widowhood and the anonymity that holy cities offer. We heard of a case of a woman who had fled home due to domestic violence and had come to Vrindavan. She had no identity documents with her. She first chose to live with another man for security. Since he refused to marry her, she took shelter in a widow's home as she could not think of any other viable option for survival.

Sensitising society on topics like gender equity and the rights of women to own property, manage their own finances and make choices about their sexuality, and mobility is essential. It is a work in progress, especially since a lot of women internalise patriarchal norms and their conditioning prevents them from attempting to be independent.

Such profiling and raising awareness might make the distribution of resources easier for those who need it the most: victims of abuse, women with special needs and vulnerabilities, and the geriatric population in particular, who have limited avenues of livelihood open to them.

Across the town, there was great reluctance to address the question of widows as a special interest group. During the interviews conducted across a wide cross-section of people in the city at random, there seemed a mass desire to render the widows invisible and inaudible. The common person on the street and the tourist, if such a generalisation may be hazarded, harbours a sentimental view of a widow as a figure who voluntarily flocks to the holy city for peace of mind and ascetic aspirations. It is assumed that this fits the stereotypical views of what a widow must aspire for. Any other desire she harbours would render her corrupt and fallible. Impossible ideals of renunciation are still expected of her. At best, she is seen as a charity case, where the rich attempt to absolve their conscience with certain kinds of donations directed at them, and these certainly are shades better than the state's response to the issue.

The boatman who took me and my colleagues on a dreamy ride across the Yamuna at dawn and dusk, was dismissive of the presence of widows in Vrindavan. He said there were no more destitute widows at Vrindavan than there were in any other city and that this was a myth created by the media. He claimed they were exhibits, to be dressed in white and brought out on special occasions as an act of pageantry by politicians, to claim votes for social service. Our boatman did not deem them worthy of any special consideration. If we had not interacted with this otherwise amenable and nice fellow, this casual reflection by a local would have been unbelievable. That's the reason why we feel that this attempt by students to conduct interviews across the town is a valuable beginning.

Do we really know what we think we know? Who is the Vrindavan widow? Is there enough research to ascertain their background and true histories?

There seems to be a general lack of interest in the well-being of widows on the whole. This seems to be substantiated by the caste and religious profile of the widows and broadly speaking, their caste status, whether high or low, did not seem to protect them from exploitation or deprivation or even from the emotional aftermath of sadness and loneliness. Health, age and finances seemed a better benchmark to understand their situation than the sentimentalised, generalised stereotype of a Hindu widow in love with, and under the protection of Krishna.

Conclusion

These faceless, invisible women need to re-enter the economy of language, identity and autonomy, in order to help them live with dignity and humanity. A PAN card, a pension, an Aadhaar, a bank account, which most of us regard as basics would be a good place to start.

These are just some of the measures which would make Vrindavan and the other cities truly a home for the widows, the beloveds of god/Krishna, so that Vrindavan truly becomes a place where love will flow from choice and self-realisation, rather than just indoctrination and institutionalised devotion.

SECTION I

Law, Policies and Schemes

Poverty has a Widow's Face

Meera Khanna

WIDOWHOOD BY ITSELF is an emotional crisis. The consequences make it an economic and social crisis for the widow herself and it becomes a huge economic and humanitarian crisis for countries with high incidence of widows, particularly young widows. In patriarchal societies, widows are culturally ostracised, socially marginalised and economically deprived.

- Almost worldwide, widows comprise a significant proportion of all women, ranging from 7 per cent to 16 per cent of all adult women. However, in some countries and regions, the proportion is far higher.
- The 2001 census shows 34,289,729 widowed females. As per the 2011 census, there were 5.6 crore widowed persons in India. Women outnumber men accounting for nearly 78 per cent of the total widowed population.

Statistical invisibility of widows and widowhood

With these huge numbers, one would think that widows would feature prominently in every policy and programme. Sadly, they are often just a footnote in the discourse on poverty.

Widows are visible culturally, but invisible in the discourse on poverty. There is astonishingly very little empirical evidence on widows. This invisibility, itself, underscores their value in the discourse for change. It can be said that there is no group more affected by the sin of omission than widows. They are painfully absent from the statistics of many developing countries, and they are rarely mentioned in the multitude of reports on women's poverty, development, health or human rights published in the last twenty-five years. The fact that they do not appear in statistics, reflects, above all, the lack of interest and consideration from which they suffer, as a result of which they do not yet enjoy the fundamental right to be included correctly in censuses.'

Why widows matter

- Many more women than men face the likelihood of being widowed for a significant portion of their lives.
- Many women are widowed when they are young and remain widowed for the rest of their lives.
- Many widows cannot depend on support from their in-laws, parents, brothers, or even daughters.
- Given that adult sons are traditionally the most reliable source of family support, young widows are economically and socially more vulnerable on average than older widows.
- There is an overlap between the incidence of widowhood and ageing among women and this has serious social and economic consequences. A large number of elderly and widowed women with not much access to income forms the future scenario.

Why widowhood matters

Widows are doubly discriminated against, as women and as widows.

- Social isolation and avoidance of widows often lead widows to miss training, employment, healthcare, education and other information and opportunities.
- Inheritance laws by tradition and custom discriminate against widows.
- The expulsion of widows and their children from a marital home leads many to homelessness, migration, refugee or displacement camps and increased physical insecurity.
- Widows are additionally constrained from pursuing education, job training or employment by mourning rites or an unwritten behaviour code.

Widows are culturally discriminated against in many Asian, and African countries. Cultural and social discrimination of widows is directly proportionate to economic dependency. **The more economically vulnerable a widow is, the higher the violation of her human rights through cultural stigmatisation.** This is primarily why cultural discrimination is comparatively less in India among the lower classes. This is because the widow is in control of her own productive resources of her labour. She may be in the unorganised labour force, but she is earning money. Among the middle class, where economic dependency is high, particularly among women who have no access to resources, stigmatisation is evident. In the higher classes with patriarchal inheritance laws, cultural discrimination is again evident.

Structural inequalities of patriarchy manifest themselves most crucially in the economic vulnerability which gets underscored by cultural stigmatisation, social marginalisation and individual vulnerabilities. It is a Catch-22 situation. Cultural discriminations result in economic dependency and this, in turn, exacerbates cultural discrimination. Economic empowerment gives access to resources. Material, social and legal resources translate as power. When there is power, social and cultural stigmatisation gets edged out. The bottom line is that it is not religious or social sanctions that underscore a widow's cultural discrimination most, but her economic vulnerability.

Gender inequality is more pervasive than other forms of inequality. Within that, widows are more unequal. Gender inequality manifests itself most in economic vulnerability.

The feminisation of poverty linked to the feminisation of household headship

There was a 39 per cent increase in the number of single women in India, the numbers rising from 51.2 million in 2001 to 71.4 million in 2011, according to census data. This includes widows, divorcees, unmarried women, and those deserted by their husbands. Approximately, 42.4 million are widows out of the 71.4 million single women. The numbers would be much higher given the fact that more men than women died during the pandemic and that there is an ongoing armed conflict in some parts of India leading to the death of more men.

Simultaneously, in India by the 2011 census, women head about 27 million households, constituting 11 per cent of total households in the country. A little more than 10.11per cent earn less than USD 75 (Rs 5,000) a month and 0.89 per cent earn little more than USD 150 or Rs 10,000 per month. Overall, 14 million households are 'considered for deprivation'.[1]

The reason why a female heads a household is not because of improving the social and economic status of women. In almost all patriarchal societies of Asia, females begin to head the household in the absence of an adult male member or when the male member is unable to support the household. This could be due to widowhood, separation, migration, desertion or divorce.

Nearly three-fourths of female-headed households are those headed by a widowed person. Thus it would not be wrong to say that most female-headed households are widow-headed/ maintained households.

The socio-economic gender bias against women and against widows in patriarchal societies places widow-headed households at a greater risk of poverty, where women are the primary earners:

- Women experience a higher incidence of poverty than men
- Women experience greater depth/severity of poverty than men (more women are likely to suffer 'extreme' poverty than men)
- Women are prone to suffer more persistent/long-term poverty than men
- Women's disproportionate burden of poverty is rising relative to men
- Women face more barriers to lifting themselves out of poverty

The 'feminisation of poverty' hence is closely linked with the incidence of widows heading households.

Widow-headed households contribute greatly to inter-generational poverty, as children, particularly girls are removed from schools due to economic constraints. Even where elementary schooling is free, girls are removed to take care of the household in the absence of the working mother, who due to economic constraints, often works in the unorganised sector and hence keeps long hours with almost no social security benefits. Girls of such households are married off early and with very little education and training, they replicate the poverty of their mothers when they are left to fend for themselves.

The vital point is that with the rising incidence of widow-headed households, it is not just women who are being added to the poverty figures, but whole families which consist of boys and girls. It will not be out of line to say that widow-headed and widow-supported households contribute the most to poverty within a region or community which is in an economic crisis.

Consequently, many studies in India show that such households are poorer compared to male-headed households as they bear a triple burden:

First, female-headed households in general have more dependents and thus have a higher non-workers to workers ratio compared to other households.

Second, female heads typically work for lower wages and have less access to assets and productive resources compared to men owing to a gender bias against women.

Third, women typically bear the burden of household chores that result in time and mobility constraints compared to male heads. This prevents any kind of training or skill upgradation.

The economic vulnerability of widow-headed households manifests in multi-dimensions:

- Food insecurity
- Exclusion from social security
- Lack of ownership of productive assets
- Poor quality housing
- Irregularity of income flows
- Lack of education
- Lack of access to credit
- Powerlessness
- Lack of access to healthcare
- Inaccessibility to legal aid
- Time poverty

If economic empowerment is the key to changing attitudes and socio-cultural norms, then it makes pragmatic sense to begin with the most vulnerable of the unequal: the widows. It makes sense to make widows active agents in economic growth.

How can the agency of widows manifest as an avenue to economic empowerment?

- Control over resources—measured by their ability to earn and control income and to own, use, and dispose of material assets.
- Ability to move freely—measured by their freedom to decide their movements and their ability to move outside their homes.
- Decision-making over family formation—measured by their ability to decide if they want to remarry and to whom.
- Freedom from the risk of violence—measured by the prevalence of domestic violence and other forms of sexual, physical, or emotional violence.
- Ability to have a voice in society and influence policy—measured by participation and representation in formal politics and engagement in collective action and associations.

How do we make it happen?

As long as we treat widowhood and widows from the cultural lens of discrimination, the empowerment of widows will remain within the welfare approach fold. But they are entitled. In this context, shifting from welfare-driven approaches to rights-based ones is recommended in order to transform mindsets and ensure that the rights of widows are protected and maintained.

How do we ensure governments focus both in policy and programmes on this vulnerable section of society?

Affirmative action by governments can make widow-headed households one of the prime beneficiaries of policies and programmes.

I. Need for data on widows

Accurate and comprehensive data on widows in India is essential to understand the scope of the issue and to develop effective policies and programmes to improve their social and economic status.

Surveys to collect data can include questions on widows' demographic profiles, social, economic and health status, and access to government schemes and programmes. A census on widows may be a feasible idea and this can be combined with the national census. Also, use of existing data like the National Family Health Survey disaggregated by gender, age, and marital status could capture the specific needs and challenges of widows.

- **Increase awareness:** There is a lack of awareness among widows about government schemes and programmes available to them. Therefore, it is essential to increase awareness among widows about the importance of providing accurate data on their socio-economic status. This can be done through community mobilisation and awareness campaigns.

II. Measurement of poverty

Poverty measurement is typically done at the household level, rather than at the individual level, which means that the poverty status of widows is not always specifically identified. Women and widows in particular, could be victims of intra-family disparities. Thus, when we are calculating with a human rights approach, on an individual basis, we also need to focus on these women as individuals in the assessment of poverty, formulation and implementation of poverty alleviation programmes. Overall, while poverty measurement is typically done at the household level, efforts can be made to identify and address the unique needs and challenges faced by widows.

- **Collect and analyse data:** This data on widows can be

separately collected from other household members. By collecting this data separately, policymakers can better understand the unique challenges faced by widows and develop more targeted interventions to address those challenges.

- **Develop poverty indicators tailored to widows:** Existing poverty measures, such as the poverty line, are often based on household income and consumption. However, widows may have different needs and expenses than other household members, which means that their poverty threshold may be different. Developing poverty measures that take into account the unique circumstances of widows can help to accurately measure and address poverty among this group. Living in a household with access to just basic amenities of food and shelter, but with limited access to health or legal resources, no access to income, and time poverty are also dimensions of poverty.
- **Using qualitative research methods to understand the lived experiences of widows in poverty:** In addition to collecting quantitative data on poverty, it is also important to understand the subjective experiences of widows living in poverty.

III. Need to review inheritance laws and property rights to ensure the security of widows

Mandatory registration of land and property in joint names of husband and wife. This change in the law will not help the existing widows, but it will help those who are widowed in the months and years ahead. The name of the widow will, therefore, already be on land records.

- **Ensuring that widows are legally entitled to inherit property:** In India, there are different inheritance laws based on religion and community. In some cases, widows are not entitled to inherit their husband's property. It is important to ensure that all widows are legally entitled to inherit their husband's property. In this regard, the Uniform Civil Code will ensure more egalitarian inheritance laws.

- **Simplifying the inheritance process:** In many cases, widows face difficulties in inheriting their husband's property due to complicated legal procedures. The inheritance process needs to be simplified and made more accessible for widows.
- **Providing legal aid and support:** Widows often face legal battles with their in-laws and other relatives over inheritance rights. Providing legal aid and support can help widows fight for their rights and secure their inheritance.

IV. Improved accessibility to enhanced pensions

For many widows, the Widow Pension is the only income, and this is a combination of central and state resources.

- **Simplification of the application process:** The process of applying for widow pensions should be simplified and made more user-friendly, so that widows can easily navigate through the process, particularly through the online system and not find themselves at the mercy of unscrupulous agents.
- **Increase awareness:** The government should take steps to increase awareness among widows about the pension schemes available to them and the application process.
- **Timely disbursement:** Widows who are eligible for pensions should receive their payments on time.
- **Regular review:** The government should review the pension schemes regularly to ensure that the amount of pension provided is adequate and meets the needs of the widows.
- **Increase funding:** The government should allocate adequate

funding to support pension schemes for widows, and ensure that the funds are disbursed efficiently and effectively. To strengthen this, a part of the 2 per cent contribution by companies into corporate social responsibility can be directed towards the pension fund of the government. The contribution can be made attractive by stepping up exemptions.

- **Universalisation of pension schemes:** Widow Pension for needy widows should be universal in the sense that for all widows who draw the pension, the amount must be uniform and not state-specific.
- **Widows' organisations:** The government can also collaborate with widows' organisations and NGOs to provide assistance to widows in applying for pensions and to ensure that the funds reach the intended beneficiaries.

V. Employment-linked skill sets

Providing skill training to widows can be an effective way to improve their social and economic status. It can empower them to become financially independent and increase their employability.

- **Relaxation of eligibility criteria:** Advocacy is needed to amend the Livelihood Mission rules about the upper age limit for those who can receive livelihood training (we suggest age 55) and the education qualification should be lowered for all widows. For various trade and occupational training programmes, the applicants must have passed class 10. For some programmes, a person who has passed class 8 is also eligible. There is nothing lower. Many widows could benefit if the rules were made more 'widow-friendly'.

VI. Convergence of schemes: Single Widow Cell

The Government of India has various schemes like National

Urban Livelihoods Mission, National Rural Health Mission, Ayushman Bharat, Mudra Yojna, Indira Gandhi National Widows Pension among others that can impact the lives of widows effectively. Convergence of various schemes can make the process more user-friendly for widows. This can be done by integrating various existing schemes and programmes for widows at the central and state levels under a single window system. This will not only simplify the process for widows to access the benefits, but also reduce duplication and ensure that they are not left out of any scheme.

Grievance redressal mechanism can address the issues that widows may face while accessing the benefits. This can be done by setting up a dedicated helpline or a portal where widows can register their complaints and get them resolved in a time-bound manner.

Policy discourses on poverty and the inclusion of women as active agents in managing poverty are more than two decades old. But we need to work and advocate to put single female-headed households squarely in the centre of this discourse on poverty and the interventions to eradicate it. This can and will be achieved by the empowerment of the widows heading the households. Widows are a most vulnerable group whose needs have to be addressed if poverty has to be eradicated.

Photo Courtesy: MA DHAM

Government Initiatives on Basic Needs of Widows

Samriddhi Pendharkar

THIS ESSAY IS on the policies initiated by the Government of India and analyses the levels at which these policies are helping the widows. In India, widows form a large, yet unseen and marginalised section of society. Over the years, many reforms and policies have helped widows directly or indirectly uplift their status. Shunned and treated as a dehumanised entity in the major narrative, these widows are reduced to the status of beggars in cities like Vrindavan.

This paper attempts to answer the following questions:

- Do government policies actually help widows in their overall empowerment?
- Do these policies only ensure the bleakest financial support?
- Do they take into consideration other aspects of human survival?
- Do these policies work exclusively for widows, or do they categorise widows under some blanket term for marginalised women?

- What steps are being taken to ensure that every widow irrespective of her class, caste and age is availing the said policies?
- How are illiterate widows with no access to technology supposed to know whether they fulfil the criteria for a certain policy?
- What about widows who neither have a bank account nor any support to help them open one and avail the benefits?
- How are institutions like Bhajan Ashrams helping?
- What about the mental health of the widows who have been traumatised?

Policies and schemes

Many government ministries are putting into action a number of programmes that cater to the basic needs of widows through the State and UT administrations. There are widow-specific programmes in addition to those that serve a larger portion of the population, which includes widows. Some of these are:

- **Indira Gandhi National Widow Pension Scheme:** Launched by the Ministry of Rural Development, the Indira Gandhi National Widow Pension Scheme suggests that any widow who is at least 18 years old and who meets the requirements established by the Government of India from time to time and falls within the category of those living below the poverty line is eligible to benefit from the programme. The National Social Assistance Programme (NSAP) includes it.
- **Vidhwa Pension Yojana:** The government offers financial support in the form of monthly pensions to women who have lost their husbands through the Vidhwa Pension Yojna. This enables them to support their lives and that of their families. This is open to widows between the ages of 18 and 65 as well as those whose husbands have abandoned them.

- **Features:** A widow from a BPL household who is at least 18 years old will receive Rs 700 a month till she remarries or her son is 12.
- **Home for Widows:** Set up in Vrindavan, UP, these homes for widows not only provide safe and secure shelter to them but also provide nutritious food, health services, and legal and counselling services.
- **The Swadhar Greh Scheme:** This is implemented by the Ministry of Women and Child Development, and aims to provide women who are victims of challenging situations with a supportive institutional framework so they can live their lives with conviction and dignity.
- **National Family Benefit Scheme (NFBS):** This scheme, run by the Ministry of Rural Development, provides a lumpsum payout of Rs 20,000 to the family in the event that the breadwinner passes away.
- **The Ministry of Rural Development's Annapurna Scheme:** The scheme provides those elderly individuals who meet the requirements but were not covered by the Indira Gandhi National Old Age Pension Scheme with ten kilograms of food grain (IGNOAPS).
- **Nari Arthik Sashaktikaran Yojana:** This is implemented by the Ministry of Social Justice and Empowerment to assist scheduled castes, single women, and widows in starting income-generating ventures.
- **Assistance for Vocational Training of Widows of Ex-Servicemen:** The Ministry of Defence offers financial support for vocational training of widows of ex-servicemen, the treatment of serious illnesses for ex-servicemen's widows who aren't pensioners, and assistance for their daughters' marriage or widow's remarriage.

- **Hindu Succession Act (2005):** It was passed to eliminate the gender-discriminatory provisions of the Hindu Succession Act of 1956. As a result of the amendment in 2005, a daughter of a coparcener has the same legal status as a son of a coparcener in her own right from birth. In terms of coparcenary rights, the amendment ensures that a daughter and a son are treated equally. The Hindu Succession Act Sections 4, 23, and 24 were the main targets of the modification. There is no longer any mention of the survivorship doctrine. It gives a woman the freedom to entirely dispose of the inherited property at their discretion without needing her husband's or father's consent. However, when we critically analyse the act, we find that as an individual, a woman's identity does not exist. Her relationship with a patriarch is required to avail the benefit provided by the act. Moreover, the act also creates an ambiguity of whether or not this act will override the state laws, because the agricultural land falls under state control. Due to the fragmentation of agricultural land, for the woman, the land is available not for usage but for title.
- **Sharda Act:** The Imperial Legislative Council of India approved the Child Marriage Restriction Act, on 28 September 1929. After its supporter Harbilas Sarda, it is commonly referred to as the Sharda Act. Revised in 2006, this Act defined child marriage as the marriage of boys under age 21 and girls under 18, the positive changes included extending the maximum length of punishment to two years of imprisonment and/or a fine of up to one lakh rupees. The objective is to eliminate the evil practice which posed potential dangers to the life and health of a female child, who could not withstand the stress and strains of married life and to avoid early deaths of such mothers who were

minors. Added to this, the increase in girls' age also gives them a greater chance to exercise their agency, and empower themselves through education. No Court can take cognizance of any offence under this Act after the expiry of one year from the date on which the offence is alleged to have been committed. Apart from early widowhood due to wide age gaps, the amended act helps with the girl being empowered enough to sustain herself in the least for she is now able to continue with either her education or her skill development.

Overview of the Available Legislation, Policies and Options:

- If we view the policies and programmes passed by the government that take into consideration, only widows, then we might not come across a lot of options. In most of the policies mentioned here, we see that while the policies benefit the widows on some level, they mostly take into consideration the blanket term covering all women. This brings up the question: why is a population as large as the widows, so unseen? Lack of policies has forced them to the periphery, and consequently, they face marginalisation on the basis of gender, region, religion, caste, class, and age.
- Looking into these policies, we further find that whatever is being done for them, the monthly allowance provided is meagre, and not really enough for them to sustain themselves, thereby forcing them (the widows) to live off donations and begging. The policies do not cover even basic healthcare.
- In addition, the widows, themselves, are not aware of all these policies. Widows who are illiterate, unsheltered and forced to cut ties with their families, with no access to technology, and no bank account to their name, probably do not have the

slightest idea about these state-regulated policies.

- Moreover, the allowance provided to the widows varies from state to state. Seeing the standard of living that varies with every city, we realise that the idea of a fixed allowance, irrespective of the city, also cannot be implemented in a country like India because if we were to keep a fixed amount, we would be faced with the conundrum of how much is enough to ensure that a widow can live a life of dignity in different areas.
- Even though most of the widows have suffered a lot and have been exposed to some traumatic event during their widowhood, there is no policy that mentions taking care of their mental health. The policies that do speak of ensuring a good life for the widows, therefore, do not seem to keep up with their claim. Since NGOs work at a more ground level, there is a need for more NGOs with adequate funds and scrutiny from the state that will help widows with not just financial security but also healthcare services. A fixed shelter, nutritious food and recreational activities like meditation and singing are a few things that must be ensured to widows in every state.

The Case of Vrindavan

People say that Vrindavan accepts everyone; and that for widows, it is a safe space. But is it really? After seeing the plight of widows sitting on the roads begging, crying when we tried talking to them, can one really say their needs are fulfilled? However, we might also say that compared to the widows outside Vrindavan, the Vrindavan widows are far better off and some even seem fairly happy. Bhajan Ashrams accept all the widows, even the ones being taken care of by the state or by private organisations. They even take in women who are destitutes. They are accommodated in shifts. It means that food is served only when the widows partake in a *bhajan* singing session.

- A study on the widows of Vrindavan by the National Commission of Women states that these Bhajan Ashrams are 'simply an encouragement' for the widows to gather in the city, and for the management to convert their black money into white. Though the setup is highly male-dominated, with most managerial positions given to males, to an illiterate widow who cares more about keeping away hunger than about the underlying political and patriarchal motives, these serve to be good places.
- There are a few observations that can be made for why these ashrams ask the widows to sing before giving them food and money. In a city which attracts worshippers and has many destitute women, begging is a big problem. Singing bhajans to get food and money curbs the problem of begging to some extent. Working to get food and money rather than accepting charity helps the widows retain their sense of self-esteem and dignity. The fixed timings of the shifts in these ashrams create a sense of discipline in the lives of the widows. Since a lot of videos available online show these widows crying while singing, one can also try looking at this through a psychological lens that also gives more interesting insights. Singing *bhajans* is a therapy for these widows who have nothing to look forward to after losing everything. The *bhajans* help them to hold on to their faith, and not lose hope. Therefore, singing provides a sense of catharsis. It is a way of meditation and a means to divert their attention from their past and present plight at least for some time and helps the widows from losing their grip over reality that has been too harsh for them.

In a place like Vrindavan, where widows constitute a large part of the population, there are NGOs that are dedicated to working towards empowering them or catering to their basic needs. Their collective voices are at least heard in Vrindavan, compared to other places where they are pushed to the periphery and languish unheard and unknown.

SECTION II

Texts and Representation

Indira Goswami

Life, Narrative, and Social Change

Malashri Lal

A Personal Recollection

IN PREPARING FOR this article, I sifted through some earlier notes and chanced upon a beautiful letter that Indira Goswami had written to me from Guwahati, her hometown, saying *Neel Kanti Braja* (Serial 1976. Book 1982) or *The Shadow of Dark God* (1986)—the novel I will be discussing had been named as one of the best novels written since India's Independence. She wanted to share her joy and creativity—we had been friends and colleagues at the University of Delhi since the 1990s.

I mention this letter to highlight the significant place this book holds in her oeuvre as it is a masked autobiography of the young Indira, a grieving widow in 1969 in the temple town of Vrindavan. Much later, the famous novelist Indira Goswami, lovingly called 'Mamoni' or 'the dear one' by her followers in Assam, had a different appearance. My first impression upon seeing Indira Goswami in the 1980s was one of bedazzlement. Here was a resplendent woman wrapped in an elegant red saree bordered with gold that caught my eye. A cluster of listeners clung to her words. The soft-spoken creative writer, Indira, was addressing the causes of the marginalised and the disadvantaged. She spoke about the misguided youth in Assam, the widows of Vrindavan, and about the women labourers in industrial units.

Indira seemed clad in an aura of genteel privilege. Her dark eyes were intense with passion; her mobile expression and modulated voice entered into the crevices of the sufferings of the weak and the dispossessed. There was commitment and conviction—she saw social evils as few women of her class did. As she said, 'I try to write from the direct experiences of my life. I only mould these experiences with my imagination.' Indira Goswami, to my mind, interrogates several facets of women's empowerment in India. Foremost among these are attitudes towards the girl child, marriage and widowhood. Indira's life maps crucial transitions in a woman's life.

Biographical determinants

Born in 1942 to Umakanta Goswami, she had the good fortune to receive a high-quality education in Shillong. Married at a young age to Madhaven Raisom Ayengar, an engineer, she enjoyed happy matrimony for only eighteen months. Then tragedy struck. Ayengar died in 1967 in a car accident in Kashmir, and Indira found herself mentally and physically destabilised. In a moving autobiography, *Adhalekha Dastaveja (A Half-Written Autobiography)*, published in 1988, Indira recalls how she shut herself in a small room in Goalpara and contemplated suicide, and how her only sustenance was the memory of a carefree childhood and the letters of her father. In other words, the privileged past seemed over and widowhood had cast a dark shadow on Indira's self-image even more than on her external circumstances. In some confusion, she accepted a suggestion to choose a life in Vrindavan, the most traditional destination for bereft Hindu widows. It is not that Indira was without other possibilities. She recounts in her memoirs that two paths were before her: she could have proceeded to London, 'that land of ancient Western tradition and culture', or she could move to Vrindavan, 'the centre of ancient Hindu tradition and culture.' It is important to remember that English education for women from upper-class families in India brought an easy familiarity with the British models of education and women's lives. Widowhood was no stigma abroad, and a foreign locale could have, in a sense, 'liberated' a Hindu woman from the stranglehold of orthodoxy in India. However, Indira went instead to the land of Braja (of the novel's title) or Vrindavan.

The widow's dilemma

Was this the right 'choice' or was it imposed by a powerful internal monitor called 'patriarchy'? Indira spent two years (1969-1970) amidst the Radhaswami sect of widows in Vrindavan, entering their fold as a compassionate member but also as a researcher. The ensuing novel, *Neel Kanthi Braja* (translated by Prafulla Kotoky as *Shadow of Dark God*, 1986), is an amazing narrative combining fact and fiction, autobiography and reflection. Indira Goswami introduces the novel saying, 'I have tried to show how the mental and physical state of a young widow takes a different shape and how this change affects her life after her widowhood.' Saudamini, the protagonist, is a thinly disguised nominee of the author. She volunteers to take on severe deprivations of the body, a sort of self-purification by which her needs are so reduced that confrontations with life's compulsions become inevitable. Despite caring parents, and a supportive community at most times, Saudamini agitatedly probes and digs as deep as possible into the meaning of widowhood. She can barely remember her husband; she now has a Christian admirer she rather likes, but parental approval and social sanction will never be granted for an interreligious relationship. The father, an idealistic doctor, and the mentally unstable mother have brought Saudamini to Vrindavan to witness and accept the traditions of Hindu widowhood. This is the crucial point to remember about the novel's theme. *Neel Kanthi Braja* is about social attitudes and the inner consciousness of a woman who has been brought up to believe that widowhood is somehow her 'fault' or her 'destiny', and that she should undertake 'penance.'

The symbology of Vrindavan: Radha and Krishna

The mystique of Braj—Vrindavan—is lodged in the legend of Radha and Krishna, the divine couple who are celebrated for their eternal bond though it is outside marriage. Radha is, in fact, married to another person, so her love for Krishna is 'illicit' in secular terms. Krishna is a key figure in the epic *Mahabharata*, supposedly written in third century BC, and the enunciator—God—of the famous message of the Gita, and Vrindavan is associated with his childhood and youth. My research published in the book *Finding Radha: The Quest for Love* documents the evolution of the romantic pairing of Krishna and Radha which is based on the twelfth century poem, *Gita Govinda* by Jayadeva. Lyrical and visual, the poet attributes engagingly human qualities to the divine pair and celebrates erotic love as a manifestation of unconditional surrender. Critics read this as the indissoluble union of the body and soul wherein the erotic is raised to a transcendental plane.

Why did Vrindavan become the main refuge of widows, primarily from Bengal and its neighbouring states? The widows of Vrindavan are the eternal Radhas, seeking the companionship and protection of Krishna, the compassionate one, the *sakha* or friend. The geography of Braj with its innumerable temples to Krishna and its highly ritualistic practices gives the widows a source of subsistence livelihood, the sense of belonging to a community, the hope of being saved from the lecherous eyes of men, and, in death, the expectation of being liberated from the cycle of Karma. The elaborate mythology of Radha's life, her family, her friends or *gopis* and their amorous antics with Krishna are chalked through the sacred geography so each woman is hypothetically surrendering to the all-encompassing divine love of Krishna. It's interesting to note that the impact of Jayadeva's poem was so great that Chaitanya Mahaprabhu and his followers in the sixteenth century virtually recreated *Braj Bhoomi* on the ruins of Mathura that was devastated by the Moghuls as the novel relates.

Indira Goswami both accepts this mythology and also debunks it without losing a spiritual connect with the worship of Krishna. The tragic gap is between the imagined Vrindavan and the reality of experience. The protagonist in the novel, Saudamini, accepts, analyses and finally rejects the construction of the widow stereotype—this is Indira's message—and it is also Indira's story.

Modern relevance

The message pertinent to the empowerment agenda may be read through the tripartite presentation of three women in the novel: Saudamini, and her acquaintances Shashi and Mrinalini. Shashi is an orphaned street child who embodies the neglect that girl children in India are subjected to. The fear of violence perpetually haunts her. Even today, the subjects of female foeticide, the skewed sex ratio between boy and girl babies at birth, the education gap, early marriage and multiple pregnancies continue to be widely discussed. Indira Goswami's street child Shashi grows into an attractive woman and chooses to 'protect' herself by becoming the mistress of a temple priest. In the community, she is derided for accepting this option in preference to 'suffering' the fate of widowhood. That Shashi suffers more severely through the loveless attachment to an impotent priest and secretly harbours lesbian desires is sufficiently built into the storyboard but underplayed.

To me, it is important that Indira in 1976 had empathetically portrayed such emotions well ahead of their utterance in public space in India. Deepa Mehta's *Fire* came twenty years later in 1996 and was visually explicit about same-sex love leading to much controversy and violence in cinema halls. Mehta's next film, *Water*, appeared even further in time, in 2005, and resorted to stereotypes of Hindu widowhood. The story was set in Banaras, another refuge for widows. Indira Goswami had nuanced the widow's deprivations of body, passion, and emotion, and woven it into a perceptive text much ahead of the rest.

Saudamini's other companion is Mrinalini, the daughter of a temple owner who has fallen upon poor days due to mismanagement of his fortunes. Here again, is a topical theme—that of a woman's economic dependence on her father and her subjection to his ill-founded financial decisions. The temple is sold off—and the scion (there is no female equivalent for the word) of an ancient family is brought to penury through no fault of hers. Today, India is speaking about capacity building for women to become wage earners and entrepreneurs so they can take independent decisions. I emphasise that Indira Goswami speaks of the politics of social construction even when she is composing what appears to be material from her experience of a cultural milieu. It is not a personal widowhood that comprises the substance of her novel, but the attendant layers of this life-condition for women.

Indira Goswami's novel is highly relevant today as the problems continue. A country report presented recently by social activist Meera Khanna says, 'Every fourth household in India has a widow. According to the 2011 census, the number of 'widowed' persons, mostly females, is more than 44 million in the country.' Moreover, according to Khanna, 'Socio-cultural ramifications of patriarchy decimate widows in India into social non-entities. They are socially invisible, culturally marginalised and very often, economically deprived. This is possibly because, in India, as in many parts of South Asia, widowhood is viewed not as a natural period in the life cycle of a woman, but as a personal and social aberration, to be devoutly wished away. Which is why the traditional Hindu blessings given to girls and women is *Sowbhagyavati bhava* (may you be eternally married). This attitude to a great extent governs the social, cultural and even economic implications of widowhood.'

Ma Dham: A widow's home in Vrindavan

Vrindavan is even today a site of gender discourse, and hence, I link Goswami's narrative to what I observed during research visits to the Ma Dham (The Abode of Mothers) Ashram. The Guild of Service has created a place for elderly widows abandoned by their families and tried to rehabilitate them by giving them the dignity of a place they can call their own. We addressed each woman as 'Ma' or Mother, and asked a few questions. Almost all the women said they had been brought to Vrindavan by a 'caring male relative' and then left with a promise that they would 'soon be called home.' The invitation to return never came.

In this period of timeless waiting, the fortunate ones discovered the collective identity of Ma Dham, and found their individual talents and spaces. A vignette stands out in my memory. One Ma who looked close to eighty was asked if she would sing for us, 'the visitors from Delhi.' As she hobbled up from her seat and gradually straightened her curved back, I wondered why we were putting her through this display. A faint tune then emerged from her wizened lips and soon gathered strength and melody. Her hands started moving to the music, her body turned to dance postures, and in a few minutes, the music and the gestures had transported us to the world of spotlights and dance halls. Clearly, she had received training, or *taleem* in these genres of entertainment. Whom had she sung and danced for? In return, what favours were given and under what terms? These were research questions, but they went unanswered.

We saw before us that Vrindavan still beckons widows, and still offers refuge. But there is a difference. Civil society organisations are aware of their plight, and are active in bringing much more than sustenance to the widows. They are bringing to them, a sense of self-worth and belonging.

Ma Dham, © Facebook

Social change in other novels by Indira Goswami

Let me further say that Indira Goswami's personal narratives and her fiction offer a carefully drawn continuum of social change. Goswami's novel *Chinnamastar Manuhto* (translated by Prashant Goswami as *The Man From Chinnamasta,* 2006) is worth considering in this context if only because the title in English draws attention to a male-centred tale. Read it and one finds the core in the man's devotion to the Goddess Kamakhya enshrined in her famous temple in Guwahati, Assam. According to popular mythology, this is one of the holiest of the *shakti peethas* (powerful spots) where an intimate part of Goddess Parvati's dismembered body is lodged. By tradition, Kamakhya is all-powerful—a contrast to the helpless widows of Vrindavan. The Goddess demands blood. Animal sacrifice—frequent and ceremonial—soaks into the temple grounds. Maddened devotees smear the blood on their foreheads and dance in frenzy. This is woman's other Avatar—the commanding authority.

Indira Goswami places the story in the 1930s but the sociological implications are absolutely relevant in current times. Patriarchal traditions have often gotten away with justifications about oppressive gender practice by claiming that 'women are worshipped as goddesses', so 'what is there to complain about.' The tribute to the pedestal and the brutality at home are the contradictions that show up in social space all the time and have led to widespread protests against domestic violence. Indira probes the causes, the rituals, and the unquestioned 'beliefs' which perpetuate oppression.

Who is the man from Chinnamasta—a wandering *jattadhari* with matted locks who tries to stop the animal sacrifice and arouse a more sensitive conscience of co-existence? Indira's research into history and ethnography showed no religious sanction for the blood rituals. She was appalled by the orgies of the flesh and the gory celebrations. The gentle author and the social activist came together to craft a novel that is a page-turner. The distance between religion and ritual is subtly debated. The polemics are so embedded that one reads the story and takes away a message of respect for an environment in which a woman, Goddess Kamakhya, is the agent. Again, I am amazed by Indira's foresightedness. Ecofeminism, Green Peace and Animal Rights are relatively new slogans.

The cultural history of Assam is Indira's constant interest. Another famous novel, *The Moth-Howdah of the Tusker* (1986, English translation 2004) is set in Kamrup district. Again, the main character is Giribala, a Brahmin widow who speaks of her inner debates on liberalism and orthodoxy as she observes the transitions in society. Feudal power is on the decline but the *satraps* or landlords do not wish to yield to change. Opium intoxication, corruption, and decay seem to pervade all aspects of the land. The widow's viewpoint is an unusual approach that Indira tends to use and the moth-eaten seat over a majestic elephant becomes the emblem of the dissolution.

Public action

The politics of literature was not merely in Indira's works but was transferred to action quite unusually. In 2005, she accepted the role of mediator between an armed militant group, the United Liberation Front of Assam (ULFA), and the Government of India. Deeply respected for her integrity as a writer and a social thinker, she was able to convince the opposing parties to form a People's Consultative Group, a peace committee. She was henceforth known widely as an Ambassador for Peace and was given an international award.

In Delhi too, Indira Goswami had been engaged with civil concerns. When the anti-Sikh riots brought the city to shame in 1984, Indira's personal and professional life was caught in the turmoil. Indira was teaching then at the University of Delhi and lived in Shakti Nagar which had become a highly disturbed neighbourhood. Her novel, *The Pages Stained with Blood* captures the brutality and the distrust in the cityscape, where the fugitives and the perpetrators of crime are difficult to distinguish. To understand the complex nature of mercenary incentives for crime, Indira even visited the infamous GB Road and interviewed the sex workers who lived there.

A composite feminist

There are many more aspects to Indira Goswami's 'womanism' but instead of entering details, let me, in conclusion, sketch a pattern. As a young woman, she found tragedy and pain, in spite of being born to happiness and privilege. Performing an act of self-withdrawal, she came out stronger with the realisation of a map of social problems relating to women. Her tools for engendering social change were the written word, and later, spoken addresses in the public arena. I don't mean to codify Indira Goswami's creative journey for no gifted writer 'plans' a path as such, but for the readers and critics, a pattern stands out discernibly.

To me, Indira is a composite writer endowed with a remarkable felicity of language and expression. Says Indira, 'The language, to me, is a velvet dress in which I endeavour to cover the restless soul in its journey through existence.' The restlessness springs from an urge to speak out her commitment to the causes of equity and justice. No wonder then that the Ramayana, that epic tale about moral dilemma, should attract her as the platform for contemporary debates. In Vrindavan, she had bought a massive volume of Tulsidas's Ramayana which inspired her comparative study of the eleventh century Assamese Ramayana by Madhava Kandali. Goswami's views published in *Ramayana from Ganga to Brahmaputra* have been expanded by many seminar presentations. Around 2005, when Namita Gokhale and I were working on our book, *In Search of Sita*, Indira Goswami generously shared her thoughts on the Assamese Ramayana and spoke of how mythological women shaped current belief systems. As I have affirmed at many forums, India has living mythologies; the old stories get adapted to prevailing conditions and are retold with a twist.

The common thread in Indira Goswami's immensely diverse and rich oeuvre is the concern for women. In her person and her work, this is echoed multifariously. Despite the complex interstices, I see no contradictions—only a holistic expression of India's many challenges to women's empowerment and a gifted writer moulding them into creative form. She received the Sahitya Akademi Award in 1982 and the Jnanpith Award in 2000, the highest honour in India for literary writing, yet she remained grounded to the principles of compassion that she had embraced in her earliest works. The 'half-written autobiography' remained unfinished, as Indira Goswami passed away in 2011. In one of the last interviews recorded, Rajiv Mehrotra brings up the topics of spirituality, pain and writing and Indira Goswami says with her candid charm, 'Suffering is inevitable for a successful writer.... If I were to write an epitaph for myself, it would be 'Here lies a humanist'.'

She saw women not as a limited category, but as key participants in the journey of a developing nation. I would say that for Indira Goswami, a humanist and a feminist were identical.

This essay was first presented in the web-lecture series on 'Women's Writings in India: Issues and Perspectives' 2021, organised by Fauzia Farooqui, South Asian Studies Program, Princeton University and Rekha Sethi, Translation and Translation Studies Centre, Indraprastha College for Women, University of Delhi. It also draws upon my tribute in 'Indira Goswami: Passion and the Pain', ed. Uddipana Goswami. Guwahati: Spectrum Publications, 2012.

Widows in Recent Indian Fiction

Namita Sethi

TO CONTEXTUALISE AND trace the preconceptions about widows in India, and the injunctions laid upon them in Indian literature and their cultural representations, I begin with a brief overview of Indian classical literature and religious sources, followed by a brief foray into colonial reform and the status of widows in nineteenth century Bengal. In particular, the preoccupation with chastity and asceticism can be seen as continuous with the agenda of limiting the widows' access to financial resources, often resulting in the widow's displacement to a shelter, usually in a holy city. This article looks at widows, located both in homes and shelters and in a holy setting, in recent fictional works by Bani Basu, Aruna Chakravarti and Vikas Khanna, along with brief references to representations of widows in popular media.

In Indian literature, the discourse about widows mostly revolves around the regulation of their sexuality and the attempt to wrest away their access to property. In classical literature, and the *shastras* in their various interpretations through centuries, the widow is provided for economically, though conflicting images and prescriptions for her behaviour emerge. This broad context helps us to understand some deep-seated assumptions about widows as a gendered category within the Indian subcontinent, because of peculiar preconceptions associated only with women and how their lives and subjectivities are impacted by widowhood, in a way different from that of widowers.

Here is an example from the *Mahabhharata:*

> Any woman, who bereft of sons, lives on without her husband, that wretched woman lives no more! Without her husband that woman lives no more.
>
> (Van Buitenen ed *The Mahabharata,* Book I, p 252)

In the same edition on the next page, is a quote from the *Adi Parva* in which Pandu and Kunti discuss the benefits and rules surrounding *niyoga*: the practice of begetting a son through another man. Kunti shares the story of the widowed Bhadra, who addresses her husband's corpse and bemoans her fate:

> 'Surely in previous bodies, my prince, I must have surrendered faithful companions or separated those that were united! The misery that I have piled up with evil deeds in previous bodies has now come upon me by separation from you. O King, from this day I shall lie on the kusa grass and seized by sorrow, shall dwell on the memory of your face.'

But the epic is full of surprises. The corpse tells Bhadra to cohabit with him after fifteen days and 'by that corpse', she gives birth to sons.

In the epic, widowed women like Satyavati and Kunti continue to wield a lot of power by means of their status as queens, and through their influence over their sons and daughters-in-law. The text is replete with the dichotomy between the ideal of the self-immolating widow, Madri, and the widows who are powerful agents, albeit as mothers of sons. The ideal widow, as recollected by some of the tales that the text presents, is supposed to waste away in sorrow and deny herself all the comforts of life. However, the ones that are truly celebrated are those who embrace the responsibilities of bringing up their family (sons and daughters-in-law), protecting them against all odds, as do Satyavati and Kunti, and the latter is even elevated to the status of a *panchkanya*.

Instances of widow remarriage can be seen in the Rig Veda, the Atharva Veda and in the Dharmasutras, circa 400 BC to 100 AD (Pathak and Tripathi, 2016, p 12), and it has been suggested that widows began to have greater restrictions placed upon them in the Dharamshastras, especially around the period from the second century BC to the first century AD. Manusmriti which appeared soon after, further codified the proscriptions regarding a widows' conduct: with the emphasis on an ascetic lifestyle, renunciation of colour, pleasure and comforts of any kind, which extended to the food they ate and the mattress they slept on, and an overall tight regulation of their movement and sexuality.

A significant shift occurred with the social reform movements in the nineteenth century, notably with the tireless efforts of Ishwar Chandra Vidyasagar (1820-1891) to help alleviate the miseries of widows by challenging and re-interpreting verses from the Hindu shastras. Owing to his efforts, the government of British India passed the Hindu Widows' Remarriage Act in 1856. It could not, however, do much to change the conventions based on the assumption that widows deserve their exclusion, and suffering, and must lead lives of denial and austerity. In addition, Janaki Nair (cited by Roye, p 54) suggested that widow remarriage was initially suggested not so much from the perspective of the widows' right to happiness but to eradicate debaucheries like prostitution, extra-marital affairs, and what was considered as 'moral degradation' arising from a woman 'being outside the protective influence of husband or father' (Nair, 1996, p 91).

Aishika Chakraborty has argued that the nationalist ideology promoted asceticism and celibacy (*brahmacharya*) as an alternative to widow remarriage, but 'the image of the widow—pure, pristine and powerful—was in constant conflict with the real images of deprivation, destitution and a descent into vice.' (Chakraborty, p 37)

Despite Vidyasagar spending his own money to remarry widows, taboo prevailed against their remarrying. The remarried widow (in the nineteenth century) was even divested of her share in her deceased husband's property as the shastras allowed that share only to chaste widows. And despite some provisions being made for the sustenance of widows by both the Dharamshastras (according to the Dayabhaga school of these shastras, which was more prevalent in Bengal as against the Mitakshara practised in the rest of the country, (Pathak & Tripathi, p 72) and the colonial legal system, widows were often deprived of their share of property, both natal and marital.

The literature of pre-Independence India engages with these issues. Tagore's *Chokher Bali* (1903) and Priyamvada Devi's *Vidhwa ki Atma Katha* (1931) are some examples. What is both fascinating and troubling is that this preoccupation with regulating women's sexuality and right to property remains central to post-Independence fiction as well, which tells us something about the long struggle ahead, to change mindsets.

Bani Basu's Bangla novel *Swet Patharer Thala* or *A Plate of White Marble* (translated by Nandini Guha) was first published in 1990, but bears strong resemblances to the popular films of the 1960s about the long-suffering, self-sacrificing woman, especially in the novel's former half. The protagonist Bandana is widowed at the age of twenty-seven, and in the first few days, she is rendered unconscious by grief. It takes her a while to return to normalcy, and when she does, she notices that she is always left to eat alone. She realises that the bereaved family members eat all kinds of food, while she was offered a special meal, bland and devoid of fish. The food, rich in dairy, makes her sick and she finally refuses to eat it anymore. She is forced to reflect that:

> If a widowed woman is expected to lose all taste for food in her sorrow, a sonless mother should also be subject to the same predicament. And why just the mother? What about the father? Did the father love the son any less? ...And how was a widower's sorrow any less? Suppose today, Abhimanyu had been there and Bandana had passed away, would he not feel heartbreaking pain and trauma? Would there be a vegetarian kitchen for him? A separate arrangement?

Bandana's child Abhiroop hates to see her wear the white sari bordered with black, and suffers convulsions. It is to keep him happy that she starts wearing coloured saris again, but she finds out to her horror, that her in-laws expected her to change into a white sari as soon as her son leaves for school. Her father-in-law, who had always treated her with kindness before, also asks her to transfer Rs 50,000 (a big amount in the 1950s, the era of the novel's setting) from her husband's Provident Fund to his name. Bandana, who does not work outside of home, and has no independent source of income, refuses. She does, however, give all her jewellery for her sister-in-law's wedding, even though she is not allowed to attend it or come downstairs to avoid being seen by anybody (a widow's presence at weddings is often considered inauspicious).

From this terrible situation, and her in-laws' home, she is rescued by her uncle, who encourages her to take up a job at a school. But even at the school, the teachers expect her to eat a widow's prescribed fare at the school picnic, and Bandana leaves the job in a fit of depression and despair. The writer reveals it is Bandana's own guilt and internalising of the social norms that prescribe abstinence and eternal idolisation of the departed husband that leads to her depression. Her *kaka* reminds her of the trends in the West, and of the possibility of widow remarriage. Though Bandana receives marriage offers when she takes up her new job, she turns them down. The son to whom she dedicates her life, turns out to be selfish and ungrateful. When she finally finds Sudipto, a man that she respects and loves, her son asks her scornfully, 'Does one marry in their old age?' when she is just forty-seven years of age. He threatens to leave following which, she calls off her marriage. A few years later, she leaves for Europe, in her efforts to raise funds and awareness for mentally challenged children.

Though Bandana comes a long way from her in-laws' oppressive ways and becomes financially independent, she feels the need to abstain from any self-indulgence, cuts her hair short and dedicates her life to serving children. By doing all this, she achieves a state of asexual motherhood. That widows' existence is seen to gain legitimacy only in acts of selflessness, is still commonplace in many twentieth century representations in literature and popular culture, what has been described as assuming 'a non-biological or asexual motherhood' and as a strategy to escape charges of immorality and also as acts of genuine love and compassion extended to those who seem to need it the most.

It is intriguing to note that, in this novel, all of Bandana's rescuers and helpers are men. They are shown to be relatively more enlightened than the women who surround her. The possibility of a supportive sisterhood is not offered as an alternative and the protagonist remains conflicted about moving on in her life and finding a new partner.

Another writer who has explored the lot of widows extensively in her historical novels is Dr Aruna Chakravarti. In her first novel published in 2004, *The Inheritors*, which was shortlisted for the Commonwealth Writers Prize in the same year, she writes movingly of the plight of Radharani, a 16-year-old widow, who is subjected to a most oppressive regimen by her own father, who prides himself on following to the letter, the strict practices of Vaidic Kulin Brahmins and drives his daughter to insanity in the process.

Radha's story is set in 1897 Bengal. Her ordeal begins with the shearing of her thick hair which leaves her scalp bloody. She forces herself to fast on Ekadashi day with the other widows of the house. She learns from her aunts that she must keep herself busy with back-breaking housework even while fasting without water. She continues to hate the 'tasteless fare' served to her and begins to mutter the names of food items under her breath. As her obsession with food grows, she begins to think of it all the time and is caught red-handed stealing a bowl of fish curry on Ekadashi. This is how her father responds in the book, *The Inheritors*:

> Lifting the pitiful bunch of skin, bones and rags, he dashed it violently on the flags. Radha's limbs fluttered like a wounded bird's, then lay still. But the Nyayaratna was not done with her. Pulling the clog off his foot he flung himself on the prostrate girl and struck her, over and over again, on the head, neck, arms and breast. Crrack! The silver knob split her skull,

sending the blood spurting down her face and neck.

The blood on her face mirrors the blood that had spilt from the rough shaving of her scalp on her return to her parental home. Her father, ironically named Nyayaratna, projects the divine displeasure that he perceives in her tragic widowhood, onto his daughter's actions, calling her 'accursed.' Thirsting for water, Radha climbs down the rickety footsteps of the well in the yard. Struck by guilt for desiring fish and water on ekadashi, she loses her hold and drowns.

In a recent short story called *Satwant Chachi* in her collection, *Through a Looking Glass,* Aruna Chakravarti, the author, presents us with a Sikh widow, who arrives in a Bengali neighbourhood in Delhi after her husband, a sepoy, dies in 1944. She is described as a hard-working woman, full of grit, 'a thin, wasted form and complexion the colour and texture of garlic,' and as one who 'never gave up weeping'. In contrast, her children are the picture of health and happiness. She takes up a sempstress's profession in the government quarters and manages to keep her home scrupulously clean and tidy. The narrator tells us that Chachi, as she is called by the children of the colony, is very popular with them as she lets them eat what they like and even encourages them with the words: *'kha puttar, kha lei'* (eat my child, please eat).

Though she dresses her children well and takes excellent care of them, she herself wears only white. Satwant helps her widower landlord Bipin by cooking for him, just as his wife used to. In fact, the first response of Bipin, after losing his wife is to ask: 'She knew my tastes and habits. Who will look after me now?'

The writer draws the reader's attention to the fact that the widower is more concerned about the inconvenience of losing a full-time server and cook, than suffering any grief for losing his companion, and Satwant is provided to him as a ready replacement by the community, because widows were expected to spend their lives cooking for and serving other people (even a Punjabi Sikh widow who is placed among Bangla families). Instead of appreciating Satwant's hard work, Bipin *da* tries to sexually assault Satwant, who, manages to fend off his advances and comes crying to the narrator's mother. The narrator's father suggests that Bipin must be let off and encouraged to get married. He justifies his advice by saying, 'Because some men cannot live without a woman.' The narrator's mother responds by pointing out that Satwant had been widowed at the age of nineteen and has been alone ever since. Her husband responds that 'women are stronger than men,' to which she says, 'To hide one's needs even from oneself? Is that strength?'

The reader is left to ponder this question as circumstances change and Satwant grows older. She is next seen during the 1984 anti-Sikh riots, when the narrator finds Satwant and her daughter once again in Delhi. As the narrator visits Satwant's house to inform her about the fact that Pammi, Satwant's daughter, was fighting for her life in the hospital as she had suffered a stroke, she finds Satwant sitting in bed eating from a box of sweets, oblivious to the raging riot outside, or about her daughter's health. The narrator realises that Chachi is losing her sanity. She recalls that as a child she had never seen Satwant Chachi eat even a morsel and was always busy feeding her children. And now she could not pull herself away from eating. The narrator realises in a flash what her life as a widow must have entailed, and makes an ironic observation about what women's true strength really means in the short story:

> Women of her generation and class were socialised into an illusion that they wanted nothing for themselves. All their needs were subsumed in the needs of the family. And therein

> lay the true strength of women. In Satwant Chachi's case, it was exacerbated further by the absence of a husband and the need to ensure the survival of her children. All she had thought about, dreamed about, and struggled for, in those years was to give her children a life. She had worked herself to the bone, worn the cheapest, coarsest of clothes and sustained herself by snatching hasty bites of food between chores.

Satwant Chachi is a remarkable portrayal of a widow negotiating social expectations and familial demands, and crumbling under the pressure of a false identity in her old age. Characteristically, Chakravarti uses food and feeding as a metaphor to unravel mental states. The story interrogates the assumption that 'women are stronger than men,' when it is used to deny their natural desires. In a way, it inverts the story of the self-sacrificing widow and mother, as symbolic of the nation, as created by a colonial discourse. A widow was perceived as a burden on the family and was required to work hard as a servant of the family, reduced to drudgery in exchange for some minimal maintenance.

As Aishika Chakraborty has indicated, the widow, if she was childless was supposed to be capable of any kind of work and 'could be shifted or sent anywhere' as 'mobile labour'. Even post-Independence, popular films like *Mother India* (1957), and to some extent, *Aradhana* (1969), the widow is idealised for her capacity to sacrifice everything for her children and the country. In *Satwant Chachi*, the story begins with a celebration of a similar mother, extremely hardworking and vulnerable to unwanted advances by men, but by the end of the story, Satwant is not associated with nation-building. Rather, she is rendered incapable of responding to reality, as around her the city of Delhi lies burning and members of her community are being slaughtered. Aruna Chakravarti turns the stereotype of the sacrificing widow on its head, subtly revealing the dangers of repression, erupting in rebellion staged by the female body.

We see some interesting portrayals of widows of the royal family of Bhawal zamindars, in Chakravarti's recent novel, *The Mendicant Prince* as well. This novel is about the famous real-life Bhawal Sanyasi case, where a missing prince, presumed dead, returns to claim his inheritance from the British. The main obstacle is posed by his wife Bibhavati, who refuses to recognise him as her husband and second prince of the prosperous zamindari of Bhawal in Dacca. This is a story, among other things, of a woman who would rather live as a widow, a terrible fate in Bengal, than accept back her promiscuous husband. Here, the widow emerges as an intriguing character, sometimes as calculating and sometimes as a victim, manipulated by her brother, who has incestuous inclinations. Nevertheless, the long drawn-out legal proceedings play out the battle between the defiant (almost) 'widow' and 'the cause of a native prince trying to hold its own against a tyrannical foreign power'.

In nineteenth-century narratives by Bengali widows, the cities of Brindaban (Vrindavan) and Kashi (Benares, Varanasi), emerge as sites which offer both shelter and disillusionment. Tales and accounts of prostitution and forced sexual labour abounded, both in relation to Calcutta shelters as well as the holy cities where almost ninety per cent of the immigrant widows were from Bengal. In Indira Goswami's Assamese novel, *Neelkanthi Brija* (1976), translated as *The Blue-Necked God* in 2012 by Gayatri Bhattacharyya, even the corpses of the widows are plundered. While they are alive, they live under the shadow of destitution and death. The novel brings to light the gangs of young men in Vrindavan, high on liquor and *bhaang*, who are seen to prowl and chase young widows. Widows are given limited choices: making garlands and grinding sandal paste if they are very young, or singing *bhajans* and begging in their senior years. There is another choice—prostitution or else living 'united in prayer' with the *pandas* if they are young enough to be exploited. The Radheshyamis, the abandoned widows living in the city, live hand-to-mouth and at times their misery, in turn, drives them to violence and bestiality. Saudamini, one of the protagonists, is a widow who battles depression as well as the conflict caused by her belief that as a widow, she ought to achieve immunity from desire. The novel leaves the reader with disturbing images of Vrindavan's widows.

Vikas Khanna's *The Last Colour*, exposes the terrible circumstances of a widow's life in Kashi. He wrote it first as a short story, then as a novel and finally produced it as a film, that was shortlisted for an Oscar nomination in 2020, a remarkable feat for a celebrity chef and first-time filmmaker. The film records the celebration of Holi in Varanasi in 2013, after the Supreme Court took cognizance of the plight of widows in the holy cities in India in 2012. Before this, the widows could only play Holi with Krishna, the deity, but never with each other, sprinkling colours on fellow widows in abandon.

The Last Colour celebrates the friendship of a quiet and gentle widow, Noor, with a tightrope walker child called Choti. Choti listens spellbound to Noor's stories, who lives in a shelter for widows. She expresses a desire to play Holi with Noor, which the old widow gently laughs off. Years later, Choti grows up to be a lawyer and returns to the widows' ashram to encourage them to play Holi, armed with the Supreme Court order. She is stopped by the inspector, who remarks sarcastically:

> Oh Hoh! Listen to them so now these old widows are playing Holi! What next? Today they play Holi with colours, tomorrow they will start wearing make-up, painting their faces with colour, and soon they will want to get married.

To the reader, it seems ironic and even predictable, that the sexually deviant and sadistic inspector, who wishes to 'grab each widow by their scrawny necks and throw them out of Varanasi' should prescribe morality to widows.

New York-based Khanna has revealed in interviews to the media, that the story was inspired by the widows he had seen at Vrindavan a few years ago, who had glanced down from the terraces and windows longingly, as people played with colour at 'Banke Bihari'. He was also influenced by a widowed grandmother at home and felt compelled to share these stories of oppression of widows and street children. His book simultaneously celebrates the strides made by law and activism, as can be seen in the story of the journalist and lawyer who rescued Choti from a certain death in Varanasi.

This brief survey can be rounded up by quoting from Khanna's novel, *The Last Colour*:

> As she watched, the smiling faces of 200 strong procession of widows, now freely walking, laughing and talking on the same streets of Varanasi she had roamed as a homeless kid, she felt like she was gazing on the most familiar face in the world, like she was gazing into a mirror…Colour exploded everywhere from the dirty streets to the clear skies, across white walls and dirty walls, across the cremation ghats, and across every white saree, to forever brighten every formerly black and white mourning heart.

The 'mourning hearts' and scarred bodies of the majority of widows need more representation in Indian fiction. Their voices remain to be heard despite the strides made by women in the fast-changing economy and worldview of contemporary India.

There has been an attempt on the part of popular media such as television and OTT platforms to explore the dilemmas faced by urban widows bringing up children as single mothers and negotiating their guilt and desires as widows and mothers. Some examples include *Katha Ankahee* (Sony TV, 2022-2023), which offers an image of a successful professional woman and the mother of a cancer survivor son, who compromises her sexual morality to save her son, but feels no guilt except in the long-drawn-out last few episodes.

Even the somewhat frivolous *Four More Shots Please!* on Amazon Prime, shows a seemingly liberated character, Siddhi Patel receiving a shock when her widowed mother informs her that she is happy being in a 'mature' relationship with her boyfriend, without feeling the need to be married to him. The questioning of gender stereotypes surrounding the loss of one's partner needs more engaged exploration, especially in the context of the loneliness and survival challenges faced by women in small towns, rural areas and traditional families.

Such questions must be asked continuously till such time when the gendered discrimination caused by the death of a spouse ceases to impact the inner and outer worlds of widows.

Sarat Chandra Chattopadhyay

Ambivalences in Representations

| Ankan Dhar |

SARAT CHANDRA CHATTOPADHYAY'S literary works occupy a significant portion of the body of Bengali and Indian literature of the early twentieth century. His novels and short stories represent many aspects of Indian life of the late nineteenth and early twentieth century, and these novels can provide us with critical insights to understanding these aspects. One of them is the condition of the Hindu widow, which Chattopadhyay continuously represents. In many of his novels and short stories, Hindu widows appear as protagonists or major characters. Although these narratives appear as sensitive critiques of the hypocrisy of caste-bound Hindu society and its treatment of women, they should be read through the complex, and often contradictory, matrix of discourses and politics of colonial modernity, social reform, nationalism and religious orthodoxy, in which early twentieth century Bengal was enmeshed. Readings of *Srikanta* (1917-33) and *The Final Question* (Shesh Prashna, 1931) clearly express these complexities.

One of the major thematic concerns that emerges from a reading of *Srikanta* and *The Final Question*, as well as Chattopadhyay's other works, is the representation of the Hindu widow, primarily the upper caste-class widow. The Hindu widow is the central figure in both the novels, as well as in more than half of his twenty novels and an equal number of short stories. The widow's centrality can be gauged by the high demographics of early widowhood in Bengal due to the continuation of kulinism[1] and polygamy, let alone the appalling condition in which they lived. Chattopadhyay's representation was, however, not the first serious engagement in literature. The Hindu widow has been a subject of literary representation and public discourse since the mid-nineteenth century. Most scholars place Bankim Chandra Chatterjee's Rohini (*Krishnakanter Will*, 1876)[2] and Rabindranath Tagore's Binodini (*Chokher Bali*, 1903) as models in understanding Chattopadhyay's widow-characters.

The banning of sati in 1829 did nothing to ameliorate the conditions of upper and middle-class widows, whose conditions are aptly expressed in an anonymous article, *Satidaha,* published in *Bangadarshan* in 1877. 'In the past, they would burn in a day, now they burn every day. Then they could burn themselves to death—even now they burn, but they can no longer die' it read, quoting Chowdhury. The Hindu widow again entered the political arena with the passing of the Widow Remarriage Act in 1856, and the Age of Consent debates of 1890-92. The orthodox group vehemently tried to withdraw the bestowal of conjugal rights to widows, who were traditionally subscribed to *pativratya* and *satitva*.

This imposition of chastity is better understood with a study of masculinity, femininity and conjugality in colonial Bengal. For the colonised subject, the masculine public sphere of rights, nationhood and citizenship was an endangered one. This public domain gained significance by contrast with, and in opposition to the private realm of emotions, inequality and 'natural' subjection. But colonialism hardly allowed the 'native' male to exercise his rights in the public sphere. His attention was then focused on the domestic space which he felt he had an exclusive right to fashion. The conjugal space was constructed defensively by the *bhadralok* as a sanctified space where the widow's sexuality was straitjacketed, an ascetic code was maintained, and she was confined within the *antahpur*.

These questions were very much alive in the early part of the twentieth century when Chattopadhyay was writing, and can be seen in Rajlaksmi's and Kamal's engagement with the code of 'chastity' imposed on them. Rajlaksmi in *Srikanta* and Kamal in *The Final Question* vitally clash against the rigid code of chastity imposed on them. Meenakshi Mukherjee effectively sums up the duplicity of the patriarchal Hindu system when she writes:

> The English word 'chastity' is applicable to men and women, but *satitva* or its equivalent in most Indian languages is applicable to women alone. The absence of a term for male constancy is a reflection of Indian social values.

A similar critique is evident in Sarat Chandra Chattopadhyaya's character, Abhaya in *Srikanta*, Book II when she rejects the word *brahmacharya*[3] as applied to the widow's code of conduct. She says:

> Everything is in a name. What in the world is more powerful than the word? Give the biggest lie the label of truth and it will become sacrosanct. Men, women and children will adapt their thoughts, feelings and perceptions to it and tread the groove for centuries to come.

The 'fulfilment' of love affairs or remarriage of his widow-heroines, Chattopadhyay proceeds very ambivalently. Despite repeated attempts and varied reasoning, Srikanta and Rajlaksmi are unable to marry each other. This trope is also present in his other novels, where Savitri (*Charitraheen*, 1917), Rama (*Pallisamaj*, 1916) and Nilima (*The Final Question*) resign themselves from remarriage. Chattopadhyay's refusal to confer conjugality on a widow and avoiding 'a happy ending' can be understood from multiple perspectives.

First, it realistically portrayed the condition of widow remarriage in early twentieth-century Bengal, where it was confined to an upper and middle-class, urban minority. The 1856 Act legalising widow remarriage and Ishwar Chandra Vidyasagar's crusade were still a failure, almost half a century later.

Second, Chattopadhyay was heavily influenced by the concept of *prema bhakti*, extolled in Gaudiya Vaishnavism in Bengal. According to it, the best human analogy of devotion is *parakiya prema*[4] or illicit love, like the love of Radha for her beloved Krishna. In most of the Krishna-*bhakti* narratives, Radha is not depicted as the wife of Krishna—she is either a maiden or the wife of another cowherd. In Vaishnavism, the highest ideal is *prema*[5], or pure love—valued for its own sake and beyond any consideration of loss and gain. *Prema* is exemplified in Radha's love for Krishna. This found rich expression in the literature of Jayadeva, Vidyapati and Chandidas, among many others. They speak of Radha's yearning for Krishna, the ecstasy of their union, the agony of her separation from him and her elevation to the level of the divine. The *śṛṅgāra rasa* and *karuna rasa* as developed in their poetry, profoundly influenced the concepts of love and conjugality in the writings of Chattopadhyay and many of his contemporaries.

Radha's love for Krishna evolved through several stages—*purva-rāga* (the dawn of love), *anurāga* (love), *mān* (misunderstanding or conflict), *viraha* (separation), *mān-bhanjan* (reconciliation), and *bhava-sammilan* (spiritual union). These stood as models for Indian writers in depicting love and conjugality in their works. However, the greatest Vaishnava poetry was inspired by Radha pining (*viraha*), after Krishna left Vrindavan for Mathura, never to return. Radha bore grievous personal loss for the sake of the deliverance of the world, a loss which she sublimated by merging herself in Him. *Viraha*, of which *bhava-sammilan* forms an inseparable part, thus becomes a separation which is not a separation. Sorrow becomes its own reward; it is the deepest realisation of the self and a means of achieving union with one's beloved/god. This is the trope that Chattopadhyay works on in the relationship between Srikanta and Rajlaksmi (and almost the entire Book IV).[6]

Finally, Chattopadhyay's engagement with the condition of widows was in consonance with his readers' beliefs and opinions, which were mostly formed by the educated middle class or the *bhadralok*. He decided to provide a sympathetic comprehension and representation of a social problem, but not a radical solution. In many ways, he typified the ambivalence of his readers, who had compassion for the exploited, but were reluctant to disturb the social order in which they had a vested interest.

The ambivalence of Chattopadhyay and the educated Bengali middle class can be further understood by an examination of the social and political developments of the early twentieth century. The development of the nationalist movement, primarily the Swadeshi Movement, and its adoption of the mythology and iconography of the Hindu goddesses of Durga, Kali and Chandi into the creation of the symbolic image of 'Mother India' deeply influenced the discourses around Indian women and widows. The popular reception of the nationalist Swadeshi ideology constructed around the worship of women as Mother Goddess and Mother India revived the arguments of the orthodox section which had opposed the abolition of sati and widow remarriage in the earlier century. In the nineteenth century, it was the chastity of Hindu wives and widows which was the sanctuary of Hindu tradition and religion. In the twentieth century, the same chastity of women became a bulwark for anti-colonial and anti-imperialist struggles. Radha Kumar notes:

> The association of Durga with 'Mother India' and the increasing use of Kali to sanction violence in a struggle for independence from colonial rule, moreover, can be read as turning the threat contained in these figures away from the self (of the Hindu male), and directing it instead against the 'other' of the Western colonizer.

As the image of the widow is appropriated and reformulated within the 'national identity', the reluctance of Chattopadhyay and his readers to disturb this image of the desexualised widow can be read as a tacit agreement between the male author and reader (subject) upon the widow (object) in literature.

The Final Question is not only divorced from these tendencies outlined here, but also from the entire corpus of Chattopadhyay's earlier works. He had consistently engaged with the unequal and exploited status of women, both inside and outside marriage. But, in *The Final Question*, he questions the institution of marriage itself; its validity and utility. Kamal does not remarry, not because of any external obstruction or moral consideration, but because of her disbelief in conventional notions regarding love, marriage and sexual fidelity. Using the dialogic mode, she unsettles, and is able to deconstruct the categories of belief and experience, one that all of Chattopadhyay's earlier widow characters have struggled against.[7]

Chattopadhyay creates his widow characters outside the ambit of domesticity to emancipate them, and yet is unable to break free of the holds of orthodoxy and tradition. Kamal is a nonconformist and does not believe in morals and institutions; Rajlakshmi is a courtesan and Kamal Lata in *Srikanta*, Book IV is a Vaishnavite nun, who has relinquished material life and domesticity. Yet, all three enact traditional roles in cooking for men, looking after their daily needs and nursing them in illness. Rajlakshmi and Kamal almost follow an ascetic code, eating only coarse food once a day, having minimum needs, and most importantly, remaining sexually chaste. It seems Chattopadhyay and his characters display the deep assimilation of the code of *brahmacharya* that was part of the code of conduct of women and widows, especially in Bengali households. Although his novels engage and criticise this 'othering' of widows, his treatment of the subject reflects the reluctance to deconstruct established social mores. This ambivalence and reluctance to offer radical alternatives is often sublimated by the widow's spiritual development and an eschewal of a material lifestyle.

Chattopadhyay's sentimental treatment of the subject of widows in his novels (except in *The Final Question*) and a sympathetic representation of their selves, may present him as a crusader for widows and women. However, his reluctance to create alternative ways of life for them can be read as a male author's compromise with the larger social and political currents of early twentieth-century colonial Bengal. His idealisation of the widow characters and deep incorporation of Vaishnavite philosophy present his literary work as a problematic praxis of his ideologies. Yet, this, to an extent, also explains his immense popularity at a time when the readership wanted only a critique of society, but not a change. Chattopadhyay had persistently explained that his purpose was not the reform of society; as a writer, he wrote of human problems but could offer no solutions to them.

An extract from *Pandit Mashai* (1917) adequately sums up Sarat Chandra Chattopadhyay's stand: that one must belong to the structure in order to criticise it. Too far-fetched criticisms do not achieve the goals that were envisioned. The two friends, Keshav and Brindavan, have both been trying to run schools for poor children in their respective villages. While Brindavan is successful, Keshav's school is a failure. Brindavan advises Keshav:

> If you reject the beliefs of the village people as superstition, how will you make them trust you?... it is not enough to have a kind heart and willingness to help people. You must be able to share the life of the people whom you want to help. If you go too far ahead of them in your knowledge and belief they will not understand you, nor will you be able to reach them.

Widows in Indian Advertising

Ruchika Bhatia

ADVERTISING CAN BE described as the use of certain strategies to inform consumers about the various goods and services offered in the market. It is a means of influencing the buyers' selection or purchasing decisions to persuade them to buy those goods. Advertising can be used for a variety of things, including promoting products for sale, enhancing brand recognition, and spreading awareness of a social cause. Advertising can influence attitudes towards a social issue by using its creative capacity to spread awareness. Through imaginative storytelling and emotional appeal, the messaging is made more effective and persuasive for a target audience. But, concerns of widows have long gone unaddressed among all the other social causes promoted through advertising. Perhaps there are no lucrative opportunities for advertisers to promote anything here, so the sufferings of widows continues to be an abandoned cause in the Indian social advertising sector.

Although the challenges of widowhood have been thoroughly examined in several literary genres, it appears that little attention has been paid to how Hindu widows are portrayed in daily life, particularly in the field of advertising. The image of the Hindu widow has been crucial in Indian literature, but their woes remain unheard in the real world. Widows have been represented in multiple ways—as child widows, older widows, transgressing widows, widows in love, remarrying widows or as frigid and devout widows. Hitherto, the representations of widows in India affirms the traditional dependence of women on men, deprived of which women can face a menacing risk within the social order. While widows may have evoked empathy in poets and storytellers, they have been a no-sell for the usual commercial ad-maker. The perception of a widow as a symbol of misfortune and evil seems to have endured. While widow remarriage was typically fiercely condemned in the past, opinions have since, softened. Although more among the general populace has become more receptive of widows, yet a full understanding of their situation is still lacking. This social ostracism often stems from the misplaced belief that the woman was responsible for the untimely death of her husband and is, therefore, declared evil and a harbinger of bad luck. The social exclusion and abandonment of widows of all ages has, therefore, led to an increase in exploitation.

In the nineteenth century when Europeans and Christian missionaries questioned the horrifying act of Sati, in which a woman was forced to immolate herself on the pyre of her deceased husband, widowhood as a social ill came to light. This compelled young Indian intellectuals to critically examine this cultural practice and question the social norms that forced widows to either sacrifice themselves or live a life of depravity. It was a turning point for women's emancipation when Indian reformers like Raja Ram Mohan Roy and Ishwar Chandra Vidyasagar fought to end the practice of Sati and legitimise widow remarriage. In literature, widows have been characterised as weak, devalued in the family structure, and forcibly abandoned on the streets to endure a life of arduous hardship. Their depreciated life turned into a tale of rejection and loneliness. They are stripped of any means to survive in a dignified way and are left on the streets to fend for themselves. The ramifications of such social ostracisation prevents them from enjoying any social or sexual freedom and violating social norms.

As a recourse to such a difficult situation, widows congregated at places like Vrindavan, in Uttar Pradesh, due to its religious significance. After being stripped of any social identity, these women are imposed with a new identity—that of the 'widows of Vrindavan.' The unique feature of this new identity is that now deprived of any male guardianship, these women find protection in their collective experience of widowhood. Whether the shared experience of suffering from cruelty really helps in any way in continuing to live is a potent question which remains unanswered. These women appear to be largely forgotten after being discarded at these religious centres, making them unsuitable in today's consumerist society.

From the perspective of feminist engagement with religion, the lived realities of these widows are still largely unexplored. These widows congregate at Vrindavan, home to the presiding deity Krishna, in the hopes that Divinity would somehow come to their rescue and save them from their sorrows.

How feelings of piety interject with their experiential realities as they are forced to beg for their basic needs of survival perhaps kills the very naive faith these women entrust in Divinity. But neither their fight to coexist, not even their divine refuge is given any space in advertising campaigns. This is because the world of advertising is propelled by achieving targets and making money; unfortunately, widows do not configure as consumers of any profitable product which could trigger sales. They do not exist as a social, consumerist group and there is total oblivion towards their existence. This, in itself, serves as yet another mode of silencing their voices. Advertising enjoys mass reach and is pivotal in informing and influencing the decisions of the masses, but the neglect of widowhood demonstrates their abject status even today.

Widows in India have long remained a symbol for a woman stripped of her sexuality, who must dedicate her life to the service of others. This preconceived idea of a gentle, self-sacrificing woman, untouched by any desire or ambition appears an unappealing model for the advertising market. The advertising industry thrives on promoting desires and ambitions, and propagates a life of aspirations and upward social mobility. Hence, any category that appears self-sufficient and disenchanted with a life of growth is an unsuitable category for advertising space. Indian widowhood thrives within the ambit of self-denial, and is expected to renounce all physical or sexual desires in favour of spirituality, which is opposite to the Western world of materialism. As the two worlds collide, the consumerist side rejects the trope of widowhood as unequipped to promote any material dreams. Also, the cultural codes dictate that a widow should be seen as a symbol of repressed sexuality, whereas advertising actively portrays women as sex symbols and objects of desire. While objectification of women for any purpose is objectionable, yet in the consumerist world of male voyeurism, a woman is constructed as an object of gaze and male attention. The introduction of a widow may help balance this distinctively patriarchal arrangement, but denying an entry confirms that the industry is lopsided.

In Indian advertising, widows and divorced women have

always received scant attention. Jeevan Bima Policy advertisements from Life Insurance Corporation (LIC) of India, which are designed to persuade viewers to purchase life insurance policies, are the only ones in India that feature widows.

In a 2006 commercial, available on YouTube, an elderly widow marries her young daughter and claims that her husband had fulfilled all his obligations during his lifetime by purchasing life insurance. The monetary benefits that the bereaved family receive, which support them throughout their life, quickly replaces the post-death trauma. The commercial's punchline, '*Jindagi ke saath bhi, jindagi ke baad bhi*,' delicately portrays the widow as a dependent who, in the absence of financial assistance, would eventually have succumbed to life's hardships. Despite the veracity of the statements, they lessen the widow's chances of being accepted back into society and achieving any prospects of personal growth. She needs support from others in order to be able to sustain her family, and the only way she can live a dignified life is by giving herself away and taking care of the kids who are left behind. A traditional Hindu widow is supposed to efface herself for the benefit of others.

Another Policybazaar TV ad from 2017 highlights the challenges a wife must face after her husband's untimely demise. The young wife seeks to speak with a shaman who promises to converse with the deceased husband at the beginning of the commercial. One can view the ad on YouTube.

The TV spot mocks the husband's inability to accept responsibility by having the wife wish to talk to her deceased spouse only to learn about the insurance documents. The advertisement opens in a traditional nighttime setting with a scarlet tapestry covering the walls and a table laden with tools used by psychics, such as tarot cards and crystal orbs. The psychic claims to be able to summon the dead to provide answers to queries. The popular image of a psychic calling upon apparitions for serving the purpose of divination is a tested example of ridicule and scorn. When a wife discovers that her husband neglected to purchase life insurance term papers while he was still living, she becomes enraged at her partner for being careless, forgetting that he is no longer alive; and nor can he be held accountable. The effort at humour is evident in the idea of a wife chastising her departed husband, but it fails. The relevant questions of how the wife would provide for the household and the orphaned 'girl' child are left unanswered as the commercial comes to an end. Here, the issue of widowhood is portrayed flippantly because of the use of stereotypical images and clichéd narratives; yet this ridicule highlights how lightly society views the plight of widows in India. The ad clearly falls short of any thoughtful depiction of the struggles of widowhood.

Since the advertising industry is driven by social norms, it is compelled to show what society accepts and what it does not. In the real world, a widow has bleak chances of remarriage and this is often replicated in the advertising world. It was only in 2013, that an ad agency, Lowe Lintas took a bold step in portraying the issue of remarriage. The ad clip shows a bride dressed in traditional attire, and being adorned with bridal jewellery. The commercial was created for Tanishq's range of bridal jewellery. The campaign managed to earn the empathy of its target audience, who viewed the ad as a trend-setter challenging the tabooed subject of remarriage. Of course, the rampant increase in matrimonial websites and classified matrimony ads in newspapers are propellers for this change, but both the brand Tanishq and the creative agency garnered much support from viewers for being progressive in their outlook. This exemplary advertisement positively reinstated the brand image of Tanishq as 'Bold, hence it is beautiful!' It was reported by *Livemint* that Tanishq was possibly the first-ever brand to introduce the issue of remarriage in the Indian advertising market.

YouTube watchers went ahead and acclaimed the ad for using a dusky model instead of the customary fair maidens favourably promoted by the matrimonial industry. Surely, both must be congratulated for their success at promoting an inspirational message, yet, the interesting point is that the commercial keeps from disclosing the status of the ex-husband, dead or alive. The question of remarriage is already revolutionary and taking up the added burden of widowhood may garble the message. To this day, widow remarriage is a concept that is socially frowned upon, and divorced women are viewed as morally dubious outsiders. In this regard, widows are often seen as non-existent and thus cannot be offered any representation in advertising.

In all these portrayals, widows are either seen as burdened with the prospect of living a complete life or as categories of non-serious engagement. These women are not given any avenues of empowerment or representation where they can fully articulate their turmoil. Widowhood in India is stigmatised on various frontiers: religious, social, and moral, and until this stigmatisation persists, these marginalised women have no scope of finding a space at the centre. They will continue to be undervalued and excluded solely for who they are. In raising awareness of their day-to-day struggles, and in promoting more sympathetic social attitudes towards those who are abandoned without a fault of their own, advertising can play a key role. Knowledge is power, as is often wisely put, and knowing about such women could help in building both a positive image of the widows in India, and garner the necessary support in their name. The adverisement industry should stop neglecting the category of the widows as a non-consumerist entity. Instead, it must be receptive towards a more holistic and positive representation of these women who are an equal part of our society as any other.

SECTION III

Social and Cultural Contexts

A Sociological Understanding of Widowhood in India

| Vasiraju Rajyalakshmi |

THIS ARTICLE ATTEMPTS to understand in a sociological context, widowhood within the intricate cultural and religious context of India and throws light on the complex situations of widowhood across regions and social strata through an exploration of the significance of marriage and the profound repercussions of widowhood. The article outlines how widowhood shapes and is shaped by Indian society.

Introduction

Widowhood, a profound yet intricate facet of Indian society, is a subject that unveils layers of historical, cultural, economic, and gender-based complexities. Rooted in the deeply ingrained institution of marriage, widowhood in India has been profoundly influenced by religious beliefs, traditional practices, and socio-economic paradigms. This article provides a sociological analysis of widowhood in the Indian context, unravelling its significance within the framework of marriage and its impact on the lives of women.

In India, marriage carries immense cultural weight, and is often seen as a union not just of individuals but also of families and communities. The institution of marriage is deeply intertwined with social and economic considerations, affecting not only the couple, but also their extended networks. Amidst these considerations, the transition from wife to widow emerges as a pivotal, life-altering event. The experience of widowhood varies across diverse regions, religious groups, and socio-economic classes.

This article seeks to analyse the implications of widowhood on women's lives, considering its various dimensions. Widows in India have historically faced stigmatisation, marginalisation, and restricted access to societal participation due to entrenched cultural and often religious norms.

Widowhood also intersects with economic vulnerability, especially for women from disadvantaged backgrounds. The absence of inheritance rights and limited access to resources can trap widows in endless cycles of poverty and dependence.

Through this exploration of widowhood within the Indian context, this article seeks to contribute to a broader sociological understanding of the intricacies surrounding marriage and its aftermath.

Significance of marriage for women in India

Marriage occupies a pivotal position in the Indian societal fabric, wielding profound cultural, social, and religious implications that define the trajectory of a woman's life. It orchestrates a transition that resonates beyond the individual realm, binding families and communities in a social embrace. Notably, Hindu matrimonial rites are dominated by rituals, like the sacred '*Saptapadi*, symbolising shared life voyages and underscoring a marriage's sanctity. Beyond its ritualistic dimension, marriage signifies a transformative life juncture for women, often associated with a transition from natal to conjugal homes, ushering in new roles, responsibilities, and expectations tethered to prevailing societal norms.

Cultural practices across diverse Indian regions further accentuates the multifaceted significance of marriage. In South India, the *mangalsutra* assumes paramount importance, symbolising marital commitment through its distinctive design and ritualistic tying.[1] This practice embodies a woman's marital status in a tangible emblem, transcending linguistic and regional boundaries. In the northeastern state of Assam, the '*Biya* ceremony involves the bride adorning herself with traditional jewellery gifted by her in-laws, signifying her assimilation into their lineage.[2]

Additionally, the grandeur of North Indian weddings, exemplified by the intricate *Haldi, Mehndi,* and *Sangeet* ceremonies, celebrates the union through a confluence of music, dance, and artistic expression, reflecting the region's exuberant cultural tapestry and the celebration over the transition of a woman from being unmarried to becoming married.

In Rajasthan, the *Palla Dastoor* tradition holds significance, wherein the groom presents a gift to the bride's brother as a gesture of respect and appreciation. These gifts and the rise in status of a woman by virtue of her marriage indicate the importance of the event in the life of an Indian woman.

Several other examples further this notion of the increased importance of a woman who is married. Prior to marriage, a woman's identity is closely tied to her natal family, and while she may enjoy certain freedom, her societal roles can be circumscribed. Post-marriage, her social status frequently experiences a notable ascent.

In various communities, for instance, marriage is viewed as a rite of passage that bestows increased social recognition and respect upon women. In some traditional settings, a woman's marital status is deemed crucial for her inclusion in certain community decision-making processes and festivities. Her participation in local gatherings or councils may amplify after marriage, as she assumes the role of a spouse and enters discussions previously reserved exclusively for married individuals.

Marriage facilitates a woman's integration into the broader social fabric. The respect accorded to her as a daughter-in-law or wife can translate into greater acknowledgement within her marital community. Religious rituals, such as *Grihapravesh* (welcoming a bride into her new home) post Hindu weddings, symbolise her elevated status and acceptance within the household. Her participation in religious and cultural activities may thus intensify post-marriage. She could take on roles in organising family rituals and ceremonial events, or even hold leadership positions within local women's associations. The *Laxmi Puja* tradition during Diwali, where married women are venerated for their roles in prosperity and well-being, exemplifies the heightened social recognition bestowed upon them after marriage.

The transition from pre- to post-marital life often brings with it increased visibility, respect, and influence within her immediate and extended social circles, reflecting the intricate interplay between individual empowerment, cultural norms, and the institution of marriage.

The institution of marriage in India transcends beyond the personal union, metamorphosing into a tool for cultural amalgamation, religious veneration, and socio-economic anchorage, ultimately framing a woman's identity.

Widowhood and its impact

The common term for a widow in India is *vidhavā*, which comes from the Sanskrit word, *vidh*, meaning to 'be destitute'. The state of being a widow is widowhood and is a significant life transition that carries profound socio-cultural and religious implications, often resulting in a distinct shift in the woman's social identity and status within Indian society. Widowhood in India is often represented as a complex intersection of traditional norms, religious beliefs, and gender roles. According to the 2001 UN Report titled *Widowhood: Invisible Women, Secluded or Excluded*, India ranks first in the number of widows in the world and is home to nearly 33 million widows. The 2011 Census in India report states that 8.2 per cent of India's women population falls under the category of widowed, divorced or separated women.[3]

The representation of widowhood is deeply embedded in the cultural narratives that have evolved over centuries. Traditionally, widows were expected to conform to specific codes of behaviour, and were expected to wear white or subdued clothing to symbolise mourning and withdrawal from celebratory events. The impact of widowhood on a woman's status is deeply entrenched in perceptions that view widows through a lens of tragedy and misfortune. The tradition of widows wearing white or subdued clothing is an example of this perceived lower status, signifying withdrawal from vibrant social engagement and participation. The expectation of widowhood rituals, such as shaving their heads, symbolises this transition to a state of renunciation and humility born out of a sense of loss and tragedy.

This visual representation reinforced the perception of widowhood as a state of loss and austerity. Her identity, linked with that of her husband, thus continues to be linked even after the passing of the husband and she loses the right to adorn herself with jewellery and may at times be made to carry symbols that indicate her widowed status. In Kerala, for example. widows may undergo a ritual known as *Karutha Pizhinja Kettu*, in which a black thread is tied around their wrist to symbolise widowhood. The removal of jewellery and a shift to plain clothing reflects the change in their lifestyle from the adorned appearance of married women. They are expected to adopt a more submissive and obedient demeanour, and to undergo rituals such as breaking their bangles and wiping away *sindoor.* Historical and cultural narratives often depict widows as tragic figures, embodying themes of sacrifice and suffering. These portrayals perpetuate stereotypes and contribute to societal attitudes that marginalise widows.

Widows are even expected to modify their diet, avoiding certain foods that are considered 'auspicious' or associated with marital status. This dietary change is symbolic of the transition from a married woman's role of nourishing her family to a widow's perceived need for austerity. In many households, widowed women either have their own separate arrangements for cooking food or preparing food for themselves after the food has been prepared for the rest of the family.

Religious practices and rituals further contribute to the representation of widowhood. Widows are usually excluded from religious ceremonies and celebrations due to prevailing beliefs about their perceived inauspiciousness. The transition from a celebrated participant in the family rituals to a marginalised observer illustrates this marked shift. The absence of adornments such as *sindoor* and *mangalsutra*, which symbolise marital status, contributes to diminished visibility and perceived value of widows within their communities. The celebration of festivals like Diwali, where married women are honoured, may evoke a sense of exclusion and solitude for widows who were once integral to such festivities.

The elevated social recognition and respect that married women experience is significantly diminished upon widowhood. A widow's identity is thus overshadowed by her marital status, and she may find herself excluded from activities and gatherings that were once accessible to her as a married woman.[4]

Widowhood curtails a woman's agency and decision-making power within her family and community, one that she enjoyed as a married woman in a traditional setting; widows are thus expected to relinquish decision-making authority to male relatives or elders, diminishing their autonomy and voice in matters that affect their lives.

Furthermore, widows are expected to conform to ideals of modesty and celibacy. Renunciation and withdrawal from worldly desires also translates into the curtailment of their sexual agency and they are not expected to form any new romantic or sexual relationships and are instead expected to prioritise spiritual devotion over sexual expression.

Temples and religious spaces sometimes limit their entry, implicitly reinforcing their marginalised status even within a spiritual context. The contrast between the social status of married women and widows within the context of Indian society is stark and reflective of the intricate interplay between cultural norms, religious beliefs, and gender roles. Marriage leads to an enhancement of social standing, while widowhood brings about a perceptible decline in status.

The economic implications of widowhood exacerbate this decline in social status. Widows, particularly in traditional settings, face reduced access to resources and support networks, rendering them economically vulnerable. This vulnerability further compounds their marginalised status, as financial dependence can impede their ability to actively participate in social interactions and decision-making processes. They are often reduced to dependents and are left at the mercy of their marital home. This often leads to desertion of widows or their exploitation in other ways. Often relegated to the fringes of society, they grapple with limited access to resources and opportunities. Vrindavan stands as a sombre illustration, where countless widows, seeking solace, reside in destitution, devoid of familial support.[5] These so-called 'widow ashrams' have substandard living conditions and lack proper healthcare. Women who relocate to Vrindavan after their husband's death, face a form of untouchability where people are forbidden from meeting them.

Widows are thus subjected to solitary confinement in their house or in an ashram. In rural areas, widows often face 'property grabbing', where they are deprived of their rightful inheritance, rendering them economically destitute.

In Jharkhand, the disturbing phenomenon of 'witch-hunting' is also faced by widows.[6] Widows, already vulnerable due to their deprived marital status, become targets of superstition-fueled accusations of practising witchcraft. These accusations often lead to physical and emotional violence, exclusion from their communities, and even death. The practice reflects a confluence of deeply ingrained beliefs, gender discrimination, and socio-economic factors. The *devadasi* system in parts of South India exemplifies another distressing reality, where young widows are dedicated to temples as 'servants of God', subjecting them to exploitation and abuse. Widows are relegated to a subservient role within the temple precincts, leading to financial dependence, vulnerability to exploitation, and a lack of control over their own lives and bodies. Their identities are tied to the temple, and they are forced into a life that revolves around serving deities and perpetuating exploitative norms.

The trajectory from married life to widowhood underscores the profound societal contrast. While marriage amplifies social recognition, widows often face a decline in status, navigating a landscape of restricted participation, limited opportunities, and economic vulnerability.

Conclusion

The sociological nuances of this complex phenomenon are deep-rooted. By contrasting the lives of married women and widows, the profound sociocultural shifts that occur post-marriage, from changes in attire and social participation to altered gender dynamics and marital responsibilities, is obvious. To address these sociological challenges, comprehensive research is needed to better understand the multidimensional aspects of widowhood, encompassing regional variations, socio-economic factors, and the intersection of caste, class, and gender. Such research can influence evidence-based policies aimed at empowering widows, safeguarding their rights, and dismantling discriminatory practices.

Facilitating the development and implementation of targeted programmes offering healthcare, vocational training, legal support, and psychosocial services tailored to the unique needs of widows is a must in the Indian context. Promoting public awareness campaigns through media, literature, and arts can further contribute to reshaping societal perceptions of widowhood, inspiring attitudinal shifts towards greater inclusivity and equality.

Sanyasa and *Bhakti*

The Widows of Vrindavan

Vandana Madan

IN JULY 1856, J P Grant, a member of the Governor General's Council, tabled a bill supporting widow remarriage.

It was passed on 13 July 1856, and came to be called the Hindu Widow Remarriage Act.

Almost a century later, in 1955, four Acts making fundamental changes in the rights to succession, maintenance and remarriage were passed by the Indian Government.

Twenty-five years later, the eighty-first report of the Law Commission of India recommended the repealing of the Act of 1856, saying that its content was fully covered by the newer 1955 Act, and that the 1856 Act was obsolete and of no practical utility.

Given this constitutional history and social legislations that have followed in the decades thereafter, it is significant that according to the 2001 Census, there were:

- 34 million widows all over India.
- 8 per cent of the total female population were widows.
- 50 per cent of this population were over the age of fifty.
- Of the existing widows, 64 per cent were aged sixty and above, out of which 80 per cent were aged seventy and above.

- At sixty years and above, 93 per cent and 68 per cent of the widows were illiterate in rural and urban areas, respectively.
- In terms of the prevalence of widowhood, India ranked highest in the world.
- Compared to the above, only 2.5 per cent of Indian men were widowers.

More recently, according to the 2011 Census, the proportion of widowed, separated or divorced women in India is higher than for men in all states.

They together constitute 8.2 per cent of the population.

According to the Census, India's population in 2011 was 121 crore of which 4.6 per cent or 5.6 crores were widows.

These are statistical facts that every Indian should know and read about.

But I believe there is another way of looking at the situation of widows in India.

We all know and hear of how the holy cities of India, like Vrindavan and Benaras, are home to the widows of India. We read newspaper reports about their appalling living and social conditions. Cinema presents its esoteric perspective, and activists engage with them in different ways, even believing that involving them in playing Holi can change their lives.

Since 1987, I have been interacting with the widows in Vrindavan, at times closely, and at times, from the periphery. Over the past three decades, I have struggled to come to terms with the situation that presents itself in this city. Frankly, the answer should not be difficult given how all too often, we hear of the ritualistic elements of Hindu tradition towards widowhood, negative social attitudes towards remarriage, and property and inheritance disputes which push widows out of homes and to these pilgrimage spots, where they seek solace with each other while they try to make it their new home.

Over the three decades of my intermittent association with Vrindavan, I have met widows from different age groups and states, and encountered many whom have lived here from their early teens and are today in their seventies and eighties. I have also met widows who have come to live here in their old age. Till recently, they largely came from Bengal, but today many of them also come from Bihar and Orissa. According to broad estimates, there are over 20,000 widows living in this holy city.

At the Ashrams built for them, I have also met some young, unmarried women who blend into the system and the rhythm of life as this world seems to provide them with a sense of security and sisterhood. Together, these women spend their days in the ashrams singing for their daily dole, or wandering and begging on the streets of Vrindavan.

Over these years of interaction, I have struggled to come to terms with their situation. What keeps them here is a question that I have asked myself repeatedly.

Many call Vrindavan the 'City of Widows'. Ashrams have been built for them by individuals and charitable organisations, as well as by the state governments and NGOs to facilitate their daily lives. And yet, anyone who has gone to this city will see that most of these women choose to walk the streets, sit on roadsides, beg in front of the temples, sleep on house verandahs, live under stairwells and wherever else they can find a little niche for themselves. In other words, these women clad in white clothes are everywhere.

Many reasons bring the widows to Vrindavan and it is difficult to pinpoint any one, but once they are here, what keeps them here is a perplexing question. Here is an attempt to understand some of these questions from the role that Devotion (*Bhakti*) and

Renunciation (*Sanyasa*) play in the Hindu worldview.

The widows' presence in Vrindavan is a constant reminder of the social mores that govern the lives of a large number of Indians, and of which the widows are victims. Their sufferings are not easy to explain, for such suffering has to be experienced to be understood. And yet, somehow, in their frail persona, as they walk the streets of Vrindavan, they epitomise a unique blend of renunciation and devotion in a society that has abandoned and forgotten them.

In the ashramic scheme of Hindu life, or the *varna ashrama dharma*, four stages of life are defined. These are *Brahmacharya, Grihastha, Vanaprastha* and *Sanyasa*.

Sanyasa or renunciation, is the final stage, directed towards a liberation from, and abandonment of the social world, a salvation or *moksha*. The monist path prescribes a rejection of worldly things: a renunciation not only of the *Grihastha* or the householder's way of life, but also an adoption and creation of alternative patterns of existence that survive outside the world of ordered things. The two worlds are, however, not separate.

The eminent sociologist Louis Dumont, in his work on the caste system, had spoken of how the secret of Hinduism lies in the dialogue between the renouncer and the householder, or 'man in the world'. Thus, though opposed to, and a negation of the householder's ideology, we find renunciation nevertheless engages in a dialogue with the *grihastha* and 'this-world'. What makes this dialogue possible are two principles: houselessness, and a social death which the *sanyasi* consciously achieves as his way of life after great penance and ritual.

Taking this as a starting point, let us compare the world of the widow, and of the *sanyasi* to show how, though both seek the same end, yet, their paths and lives are vastly different and essentially incomparable.

Ironically, the status that the *sanyasi* seeks and gains through penance and hardship, is so easily ascribed to the widow by a society that shuns her. It becomes her only way of life, and she slips into it for lack of choice or voice. If we compare the two worlds, we see a novitiate seeking *sanyasa*, who officiates at his symbolic death by ritually destroying, himself. As D R Kinsley says, 'he ceremonially annihilates the old, bound, finite creature, who is less than divine and immortal.' He does this as a mourner at his own death, presiding over his own funeral, donning the garb of the chief mourner, shaving his hair and paring his nails, thus entering a state of liminality, only to 're-emerge' as a renouncer.

So too does a widow enter a new life through her own symbolic death, except that her state is not a chosen one, but socially prescribed. She, too, dons the white garb of a mourner. Custom demands that her hair be shorn, and her appearance made unattractive with nondescript white garments. Her body is symbolically bound in every social way to confine her to celibacy and place her in a state of liminality. However, unlike the *sanyasi*, she never 're-emerges' from this state, but spends her life living always at the edge of society, somewhere in between and in betwixt.

While the *sanyasi* consciously seeks freedom from the bonds of 'this-worldly' living or *samsara* as opposed to *grihastha*, the widow finds she has no choice, and cannot be 'of this world' because of reasons beyond her control, which stigmatise and ostracise her as a symbol of inauspiciousness.

For the *sanyasi*, escaping the bonds of *samsara* and overcoming the finality of death are made possible by not only renouncing the 'this-worldly' life through his social death, but also by attaining a state of deep meditation and *samadhi*; the widow simply 'lives' in this world, but is not 'of this world', because she is socially dead, a shadow of her formal self.

A *sanyasi* through his vows and austerities attains a symbolic immortality, and escapes the innumerable cycles of birth, death, and rebirth, attaining liberation for his soul.

A widow, on the other hand, already lives a renouncer's life, and yet her austere, *sattvik* life brings her neither immortality nor *moksha*.

There are many symbolic acts which systematically destroy the novitiate's householder status, the final of which is the breaking of the sacred thread, donning a string of *rudraksha* and carrying a begging bowl, *kamandala*; so too, the widow breaks her sacred familial bonds, dons a string of *tulsi* beads and carries her begging bowl for alms.

But there is a deep difference here. Having abandoned this world 'by choice', a *sanyasi* adopts a new status as he 'emerges' from the state of liminality, allowing his hair and nails to grow freely, reorienting himself to a new identity, a state beyond this social world and the world of his ancestors. For, through his social death, the *sanyasi* achieves his goal of transcendence, and is now incorporated into the world of renunciation. He deals with his changed status reflected in a transfiguration of his life. Besides representing an alternative to the householder's way of life, he moves to a state outside it, which is a state of houselessness, of chaos, symbolised by his coming to the forest or *aranya*. This new way of life, and the spiritual quest for *aranya*, suggesting freedom from conflict and a boundless existence may be seen as his first step to *moksha*.

On the other hand, the unfortunate widow remains permanently bound in a state of eternal mourning, caught between the social world, and the world of her ancestors. For once she is socially declared dead, she never 'emerges'. She finds no transcendence as she hovers in her liminal state. Having found that society excludes her, she must seek a space for herself and a new identity rooted in devotion to her own salvation and transcendence. The widow thus comes to symbolise a boundless, yet bounded existence in her permanent state of liminality. She too, seeks the 'forest of chaos', her *aranya*. And it is this search, her *bhakti*, that brings her to Vrindavan, the forest of *Tulsi*, the land of Vaishnava *bhakti*, the land of Krishna, her god and *ishta deva*.

Here she continues, however, to live liminally, in her socially ascribed death, forgotten by her family and society. But then, here are others like her. She is not alone in her solitude, her invisibility or liminality. Here she finds a purpose, for, in pursuit of her *moksha*, in Vrindavan she turns to the middle path–a self-abandonment to the divine—her *bhakti* to her god, her *ishta deva*—her Krishna, who will release her from suffering. While she carries upon herself the symbolic markers of her widowed identity that make her 'of this world,' yet outside of it, the widow also carries her '*deva*' upon her being.

The symbols of Vishnu and Krishna on her forehead are like the *ishta linga* worn by a devout Saivaite that symbolises his non-differentiation from his lord. As Abbe Dubois wrote, '…where the *lingam* is…is the throne of the deity, without distinction of class or rank.' And so is the case with the widow's devotion. The ideological basis of her life lies in passing from the ostracised and hierarchised world where society has placed her, towards the direct and the personal relationship between the worshipper and the god, somewhat like the Lingayat who finds peace in Shiva.

The widow here symbolises in her *bhakti*, not only a transcendence, but also an opposition of the individual to the collective. Her persona also symbolises the mobile idol that she carries with her always, represented in the *tilak* on her forehead, the *tulsi* beads around her neck, and her constant circumambulation or *parikrama* of the city. And in this wandering, her *parikrama*, she is unbounded and unfettered.

No longer a *sumangali*, she embodies inauspiciousness, but she is a devotee, and in her devotion to her *ishta deva*, 'He', her Krishna, she becomes a symbol of austerity and *sanyasa*.

The widow's renunciation becomes obvious from her selfless devotion and the desire for union with the absolute reality of her devotion and her *deva*. Her life becomes a symbol of 'forced' renunciation and detachment from the domestic, balanced by her selfless devotion to her *ishta deva* and his many forms. Her detachment or *virakti* from a 'this-wordly' existence is her *bhakti* to Krishna, and presents a dialectical unity of opposites at a higher level of living. And thus, her death, when it occurs in Vrindavan, is called *dhaam prapti*, her union with the absolute, her divine salvation, her *moksha*.

So, the next time you wonder, why are there so many widows in Vrindavan, ask yourself:

- Is it because Vrindavan is a safe haven?
- Does the safety come from the 'sisterhood' of a shared life?
- Is it because survival is easy here?
- Is it because there will always be goodwill?
- Is it, to borrow, Anne Pearson's idea, 'Being here gives them 'peace of mind'?

I believe it is all of the above, and what Jamuna ji, a sixty-year-old widow from Bengal once said to me many years ago, encapsulating in two words all the emotions of her *bhakti, sanyasa* and her *virakti*. On being asked what brings her to Vrindavan, she had replied, '*Ooni aachen*' (HE is there).

Widows and Widowhood in Lado Sarai

Tarun Sharma

LADO SARAI IS an urban village located in the south district of Delhi on the Mehrauli-Badarpur Road, and is at walking distance from the Qutab Minar. It is a Hindu-dominated area, with small populations of Muslims and Christians, as well. Lado Sarai is largely inhabited by the Jatt community, comprising 75 per cent of the total population. However, other communities like Khati, Nayi, Kumhaar, Chamaar, *et al.* also have a decent representation in the area. The place has come a long way, as Lado Sarai underwent several major cultural and economic changes over the past three decades. From being a rural area where its inhabitants heavily relied on their cattle for their livelihood, the place has seen a drastic transformation.

More than half of the local inhabitants have rented out their ancestral property, which eventually became their primary source of income. As a result, several coaching institutions and art galleries have been set up in Lado Sarai. Lado Sarai is now home to more than forty art galleries, and half a dozen UPSC coaching institutions, which has resulted in an increase in the number of people renting accommodation on an annual basis, and money has flown in at a rapid pace. Such developments have led to economic changes, giving way to a modern, more vibrant lifestyle.

This change in the economic fabric has brought social change as well. Lado Sarai was always a culturally rich and traditional space. Now, with its varied social composition, the people of Lado Sarai realised a need for community panchayats and communities like Nayi and Chamaar have their own panchayat systems, making it a unique social characteristic of Lado Sarai. They also have their respective panchayat *ghars* which look into their local issues, if unresolved, and they have the option of moving up to the panchayat at the village level.

Of special note is their traditional celebration of Diwali in Lado Sarai, participated in by almost all households in the village, including all Hindus and some non-Hindu communities, following an age-old tradition even in the twenty-first century. The tradition is to place the first five *diyas* at places of significance such as the well, temples and a very old peepal tree, and the *chaupaal* where travellers rested before they could resume their long journey. This tradition is still prevalent, and is followed by most of the local inhabitants of the village.

I was born in Lado Sarai in 1993, and have been living there ever since. The atmosphere was typically patriarchal with women expected to be the stakeholders of private life in households and barred from any interference in the public sphere. While this has undergone significant changes over the course of the last couple of decades, things were very different in the seventies and the eighties. Murti Devi, my grandmother, once told me a story. She narrated that one morning when she was at the well to draw some water, she found it difficult to place two *matkis* on top of her head, and seeing her struggle, a woman whom she barely knew offered help and placed the vessels on her head. She said that somewhere from far, her father-in-law, and my great-grandfather had seen that incident. As she was about to enter the house, he had asked her to drop and break the vessels. When she asked for a reason, he had said, 'The woman you took help from is a widow, and hence the water in these vessels is unfit for drinking.' She was shocked and so was I, after listening to the incident. This was my first indirect encounter with widowhood and the stigma attached to it. It will not be wrong to say that certain words that stereotypically resonate with widows and widowhood are: submissive, subjugating, demeaning and discriminating. This is common and true of the widows of Lado Sarai; however, times have taken a turn and so have the stereotypes.

I shall attempt to examine how the local culture and traditional values of Lado Sarai have empowered widows, both socially and economically. Lado Sarai presents a unique and not-so-common case of widows when compared to other places that do not marginalise them after the death of their respective husbands. This allows them to lead a respectable life, and doesn't expect them to sacrifice and compromise in every sphere of life. Not to say that such a treatment of widows is unique only to Lado Sarai, but considering the patriarchal setup of this village, this definitely comes as a surprise to outsiders.

A common stigma and stereotype that is associated with widowhood is that they are inauspicious and should be barred from auspicious occasions like weddings, and related ceremonies. This is not the case with the widows of Lado Sarai. Widows, whether young or old, are always invited to sing traditional and community songs before the wedding day and there is no bias based on their marital status. Another interesting fact is, irrespective of the caste they belong to, widows from all communities are invited to participate in pre-wedding festivities like the *sangeet*, where folk songs are sung as blessings for a successful marriage.

I distinctly remember my widowed grandmother participating in such occasions, where people from different communities would invite her, and this practice is still prevalent all across Lado Sarai. Another stereotypical belief is that widows shall not be seated in the assembly hall where the wedding ceremony *pheras* take place. This is also not true in the case of Lado Sarai, as widows from all communities attend such ceremonies. Therefore, the widows of Lado Sarai are not considered inauspicious at all. They are treated with respect, and considered indispensable during such occasions and festivities.

Widows are expected to live a minimalistic life with almost no materialistic desires that can be reflected in their attire, and food habits, and their status is supposed to be reflected in the way they carry themselves around. However, I am witness to first-hand experiences of certain treatment of widows in Lado Sarai, that not only make them feel like equals but also ensures that they live a healthy and fulfilling lifestyle.

Asha, a young widow in Lado Sarai, who lost her husband at the age of thirty and had two children to raise by herself, was aptly supported by the locals. At first, Asha was taught how to tailor clothes by some women of the society, and then a mutual understanding was worked out that the women would get their personal stitching done by Asha, in order to financially support her. This decision was taken by the elderly women of the society, and was supported by some young ones that allowed Asha to earn enough money so that she need not live a life of hardship and helplessness.

Santosh, another resident of Lado Sarai, lost her husband in an accident and became a widow at a time when none of her children were earning. She was helpless, but this was when the locals gathered to help her out. As a result of the newly opened coaching institutions, a lot of students who came to Lado Sarai brought business opportunities for the locals as well. One such business opportunity was that of a tiffin service. The local women started cooking food for these students who either came to their houses to eat, or would get their tiffin delivered where they were residing. The local women considered this as a good opportunity to help Santosh. Since she had very little money to buy tiffin boxes that could be used for delivery, they decided to ask the students (clients) who used to come to their respective houses to eat, to move to Santosh's house so that she didn't have to incur the cost of buying boxes, and could start the business right away. This effort empowered Santosh to re-establish her financial earnings after the death of her husband.

Aleksandr Solzhenitsyn argues in his Nobel prize-winning work, *The Gulag Archipelago* (1973) that a society can only prosper if it follows the path of truth and doesn't compromise on its social responsibility. History has shown us several examples of crumbling societies that couldn't walk the path of truth with full responsibility. I firmly believe that as a society, it is our responsibility to not only become the voice of the voiceless, but also empower them until they can stand, and defend themselves and ensure their own well-being.

Lado Sarai as a community has largely fulfilled its responsibilities towards the widows of their society. Here are more instances of human compassion from within the community that not only encourages, but sets positive examples for the generations to come.

Kela, a sixty-five-year-old woman who runs a small bangle shop from her house itself, has been a known personality for all those born and brought up in Lado Sarai. She is popularly known as *Manihaari* (a woman who makes and sells bangles), who was devastated after the death of her husband, and became the sole breadearner of the family. With no children, she was left with no option but to run the same small shop that was left behind by her husband. With time, the marketplace in Lado Sarai changed and several new and fancy shops were established by both locals and outsiders. The younger lot of shoppers from the area now began buying their cosmetics and bangles elsewhere. However, the elderly women of Lado Sarai never stopped buying their bangles from Kela, and made sure that she never ran out of business. This continued until the sad demise of Kela; she was poor but she never had to beg for food and other basic amenities. It could not have been possible without the support of the elderly women of the village, who were always certain that it was their responsibility to look after the helpless Kela, and strengthen her belief and courage with their compassion and love.

As teachers and well-wishers of our students, we always advise them to become financially independent as soon as possible. We tell them that financial independence is the key to a self-governed life. It would not be wrong to claim that it is not only our young women who need financial independence, but also the older citizens of our society. I have already mentioned the example of Kela. However, I cannot conclude my argument without mentioning Sushila, an old woman from the Kumhaar community. She earns her daily bread by selling earthen pots and other vessels in a small alley in Lado Sarai. The business never has a peak, but it was around Diwali that she could manage to save some money for the future months, by selling *diyas* to the entire village. One major drawback of modern civilisation is that we have left behind some of our purist traditions and adopted technological advancements that may negatively affect the economically lower-class people in our society. With the introduction of electrical and electronic lights, traditional lamps have been forgotten, and the business of people like Sushila has taken a big hit.

Understanding the importance of the situation, and the need to take a strong decision that may help Sushila, almost all the local inhabitants of Lado Sarai decided to keep buying their traditional *diyas* from her, and also encouraged their tenants to do the same. This decision not only helped the poor widow to financially recover, but also brought her a sense of being loved and a belief that she was not marginalised after the death of her husband.

All the narratives mentioned above are stories of compassion, love, responsibility and camaraderie, for people in the community understood that becoming a widow is an unfortunate incident that may happen to anyone, but life should not stop because of it. The community of Lado Sarai not only understands it, but also offers help and support to whoever is in need. Widows in India often face a life of widowhood that is full of struggles and obstacles at every step, however, with the power of love, empathy and responsibility as a society, the women of Lado Sarai have brought a change in the lives of many, and this can be an inspiration for others—that if we stand together as a collective identity towards bringing a change in society, then nothing is beyond the reach of people who approach all problems with love in their hearts and commitment—till it becomes an intrinsic part of their nature.

SECTION IV

On the Trail of the Widows of Vrindavan

THE ESSAYS BY students in this section are anecdotal and offer analytical insights into the following questions:

- Where do these widows come from and why?
- In which locations at Vrindavan can they be found?
- What are the perspectives of people about them?
- What are their living conditions?
- How far does state policy impact/help them?
- Reasons for their invisibility despite their prolific numbers.
- Opportunities for freedom and sisterhood.

Vrindavan's Kunj and Galis

Interviews of People around Temples

Muskan Dhankher, Aditi Chandra, U Sai Sruti, Sucheta Raj, Ishiqa Shadija, Arshpreet, Ayushi Pal

Street of Vrindavan

ON THE FIRST day of our visit, we stayed in the city's outskirts—an area characterised by narrow streets, rocky *kutcha* roads and little light. The main roads on the outskirts of the city are well laid out *pukka* roads, but mobility remains a problem inside the narrow lanes of Vrindavan. No cars are allowed but noisy e-rickshaws run amok making even walking difficult. Cows roam freely across the city's roads. There is a temple at every ten steps which gives the city its distinct character.

First impressions of Vrindavan

This is known as the 'City of Widows' since a lot of women migrate here after losing their husbands or when their family abandons them. Vrindavan gives these widows a place to stay and access to food, easily. This place gives them a reason to live and most of them become devotees of Radha-Krishna. Vrindavan is a sacred place for people belonging to the Vaishnavite tradition of Hinduism. The other prominent areas surrounding Vrindavan are Govardhana, Gokul, Nandgaon, Barsana, Mathura and Bhandirvan. All these places are considered to be at the centre of Radha and Krishna worship. Millions of devotees of Radha -Krishna visit Vrindavan and its nearby areas every year to participate in a number of festivals. The common salutation or greetings used in the Braj region by its residents is *Radhe Radhe* which is associated with the Goddess Radha or *Hare Krishna* which is associated with Krishna.

Nidhivan

On our visit to Nidhivan, we spoke to a few widows who were sitting outside the temple. They were all from West Bengal and had migrated to Vrindavan either because they had no source of livelihood or because they were abandoned and had nowhere to go. They were not allowed to even go inside the temple, but they said that they were happy because Radha and Krishna were providing

Widows outside Nidhivan
© **Ananya Aggarwal**

them with food. In West Bengal, people worship Goddess Durga but the widows who come to Vrindavan are devotees of Radha and Krishna. One woman also said that she could not re-marry because they consider Krishna as their husband.

We spoke to some of the tourists who were visiting the temples of Vrindavan. They said that they had no idea that Vrindavan is also known as the 'City of Widows'. We asked them about their perceptions of the widows and of the discriminations they face. One of the widows said that it is usually not their son who abandons them, but it is the daughter-in-law who asks them to leave. She mentioned that it is women who are upholders of patriarchy, not men. In the movie *Prem Rog*, when the widowed heroine was asked to shave her head, it was her father who asked her not to and it was the women who were using harsh words. Men care less about these traditions, but often it is women who follow them, due to society's conditioning.

Conversations around the temples and on the streets

Our day commenced with a visit to Govind Dev ji and Rangnath ji Mandirs where our group interacted with locals, pundits and shopkeepers on their views and observations of the widows in Vrindavan. Some widows were interviewed as well. It was noted that most people hesitated to talk about this topic and constantly redirected the conversation away from them. They denied the prevalence of any discrimination or abuse against the

Govind Dev ji Mandir
© Arshpreet Kaur

widows in Vrindavan. Most of them even justified the cultural restrictions set upon the widows while there were a few who also questioned these beliefs surrounding them. It was noted that most locals were uninterested and seemed indifferent and even unaware of the issues faced by the widows.

The pundit of the Rangnath ji Mandir expressed his opinion that the widows should not wear colourful sarees, bangles and *bindi*. His belief was that once widowed, these women do not have a man to be their guardian, so they should live alone, immersed in the *bhakti* of Krishna. When we asked him if these women faced any sexual abuse, he dismissed the notion by saying, '*inko kaun chhedega*' (meaning who would bother to harass these women?), indirectly implying that these widows were no longer desirable. He seemed unashamed about his views and felt that it was the only legitimate way of perceiving the widow community. He did not seem to understand the implications of what he had said. This is how women are perceived in society: as weak, fragile playthings. They do not have their own identity as the belief is that a woman's identity is first that of her father's, and then of her husband. We found this really sad, indeed.

At Banke Bihari Temple, following the *darshan*, we interviewed the shopkeepers and the locals. Most of the shopkeepers did not show any interest. A few who did respond, seemed unconcerned about the plight of these widows. According to them, the widows came to Vrindavan because they wanted to, and Krishna called them here. They related everything to mythology. We also interviewed a few policemen and found out how they felt. We came across the following opinions:

- Abandoned by their families, the widows come to Vrindavan because there is a lot of scope to earn as it is a tourist place. Alongside, they can also devote themselves to Krishna. The old ladies earn money by begging and by selling garlands for *puja* and by applying *teeka* on devotees' foreheads.

- One policeman had a very progressive approach. He said that if a man can remarry, then a woman also has an equal right to remarry, and thus she should.
- He also gave a caste perspective to his thoughts. According to him, the situation of the widows in the lower castes is even worse, especially in villages. He cited a few examples from his own village in UP.

We interviewed *autowalas* (drivers of three-wheeler rickshaws), who told us about how the widows struggle for survival and how bad the situation is for most of them. The widows are often found begging in the streets.

Most of the street widows are from West Bengal and cannot speak Hindi. This was a major issue in speaking to the street widows. One of them who could speak Hindi told us how they lived in very tiny rooms and paid their rents by the money they earned from begging. They eat at the Bhajan ashrams in which they sing *bhajans* to earn their meals for the day.

© Himanshi Chawla

Team interviewing the locals at Rangji Mandir
© **Arshpreet Kaur**

The field trip to Vrindavan was enlightening. We saw for ourselves how widows are treated in society. Vrindavan for these women is considered safe, but it is not always so. It left us wondering if there is any safe place for women in India, especially for widows. Women will keep suffering in one way or the other, unless social perceptions and attitudes change at all levels. Before our field trip, we used to think that these widows would be living happily in Vrindavan but we had now learnt the actual status of these widows.

Parikrama Marg

A Site of Sisterhood

| Sakshi Mishra |

Group of widows from different parts of India at Parikrama Marg
© Himanshi Chawla

PARIKRAMA OR *PRADAKSHINA* refers to the circumambulation of sacred places in Vrindavan's Parikarma Marg and of every famous temple on this marg. However, it is also the place where you can find 'street widows' in large numbers. One of the famous widow ashrams, Gauri Gopal is also located on this marg.

Street widows include those who cannot find any shelter or

home, and also those who are living on the streets by choice. On the streets, they can find different means of earning such as through begging for alms. Hundreds of widows have made their homes on the footpaths. On the streets, they live in groups and could belong to different places, castes, and class. But there was something very special about these street widows and that was the bond of sisterhood, especially in the way they talked about each other, and of how they were aware of each other's struggles and difficulties, especially about the uncomfortable things which even their families did not know about. They smiled, laughed and cried together. We sensed a kind of unbreakable bond between them.

Jamuna Amma

Jamuna Amma
© Sakshi Mishra

I met an old lady named Jamuna who was in her eighties. She gave this name to herself because she liked the name of the River Jamuna. Her husband died early and her own family members were dead too. Jamuna Amma was in a hurry to reach somewhere, so I talked to her while she was walking towards her destination. She told me that she is from Bareilly and had come to Vrindavan because of Shri Kripalu Maharaja's *Bata Baati* initiative. She was incredulous and said, 'To me, it was unbelievable.'

She also told us that earlier she was getting a pension but from the past year, she was not getting it because her name on her Aadhaar card was different from her real name. It could have also been because of a shift in the political scenario. The *pradhan* of her village had changed. While we were walking, she seemed to be in a rush to get somewhere and was preoccupied with her own thoughts. When I asked her about the subject of her ruminations, she said she was lost in thoughts of Shri Rama.

Harbai Amma

She hails from a small village in Chhattisgarh and declared that she had come here of her own will, chasing peace of mind. She claims that her son and daughter pay for her maintenance, but it did not seem likely. Widows from Vrindavan do not always reveal the truth and one has to read between the lines. While I was talking to her, there was a pleasant smile on her face and she even sang a *bhajan* for us. She was very cheerful and said she was staying with a group of Ammas, all of them from Chattisgarh. Their villages were far from each other's homes, but their hearts seemed to be connected.

Harbai Amma
© Sakshi Mishra

On my way, I came across local people, Indian tourists and foreigners and noted down their responses.

Conversations with local people

I spoke to many local people, including shopkeepers, street vendors, and people living in Vrindavan. To my shock, everyone's reaction was the same. I asked them whether they were aware that Vrindavan is also known as the 'City of Widows' and they were all furious. Some even shouted at me, telling me that this was the worst description they had ever heard of their city! To describe Vrindavan as a 'City of Widows' is a crime for which I would get punished, they said to me. According to them, Vrindavan is described as the 'City of Krishna and Radha.'

Conversations with Indian tourists

Indian tourists had a different view from the locals. They accepted the fact that Vrindavan is known as a 'City of Widows'. Most of them said that many widows come to Vrindavan because Krishna accepts everyone irrespective of their circumstances.

Conversations with foreigners

The only thing that had pulled them to Vrindavan was Krishna. They came here for Krishna and knew only of Krishna.

Even a brief journey had showed us how invisible the widows can be, even though they are found everywhere.

"विधवा" मेरी पहचान नहीं
(Vidhwa Meri Pechan Nahi)

| Sejal Khanna |

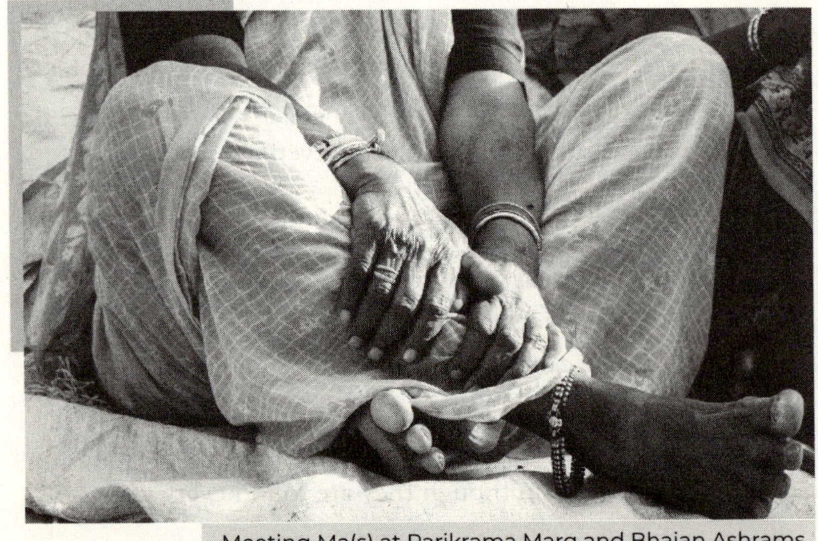

Meeting Ma(s) at Parikrama Marg and Bhajan Ashrams
© Himanshi Chawla

ONE MORNING, as I was ambling through the narrow streets and aisles of Parikrama Marg in Vrindavan, I was flooded by an ominous, uneasy feeling at the sight of these innocent souls who had been deprived, robbed of their abodes, family connections and identity. Often vexed at the sight of some mischievous monkeys who shared the same space as them, a few of the widows whisked them off from their path. The old, decayed and crumbling little houses enclosing the long, endless path echoed the woeful state of these Mas of Braj Dham.

The term *parikrama* or *pradakshina* describes the circling of Vrindavan's holy shrines. Devotees often stroll through the streets of Vrindavan through the Parikrama Marg route that circumnavigates the town. It is on this long trail that one finds the greatest number of young, middle-aged and elderly widows who stand together united in their sisterhood, despite being abandoned and shunned by their own folks and families due to various illogical superstitions embedded in the 'developing' psyche of Indian society. The agony of the widows has not changed much since Sati was abolished in 1829 and the Hindu Remarriage Act passed in 1856. The widows, who must beg for a livelihood and have their heads shaved and their foreheads covered with sandalwood, recite religious hymns, not just for spiritual redemption, but also to earn a simple, mundane livelihood. Parikrama Marg comes alive every morning with the chitter-chatter of birds, the sweet rustling of leaves, the commotion caused by the little monkeys and the chants of these women in white as they commence their daily rituals.

Monkey at Parikrama Marg
© Himanshi Chawla

Amidst the frequent conversations with the widows, we came across a surprising fact—that the city comprises mostly of Bengali women who had been ostracised by their families in the name of oppressive religious practices. 'I made the decision to visit Vrindavan to avoid having to endure this kind of atrocious treatment. A woman should pass away before her husband,' said Parul Datta, an old Bengali widow who was begging on Parikrama Marg.

A journal article by Malini Bhattacharya published by the *Social Scientist,* titled, *The Hidden Violence of Faith: The Widows of Vrindavan,* examines the words of the renowned Uma Bharti, former Central Minister of Women and Child Development while addressing destitute and poor Bengali widows. She seems to have made a localised observation about the Bengalis' penchant for abandoning their bereaved mothers and sisters on the streets, forcing them to seek refuge in Vrindavan. According to multiple local sources, the minister's remark outraged many among the audience, who reacted angrily and objected, calling it an insult to the religious vocation that had truly brought them to Vrindavan. They said that they chose to live in Vrindavan voluntarily in order to serve Radha and that they would prefer to pass away there while chanting Radha's name. In the face of intense hostility, Uma Bharti was forced to take back her statement.

The myth of 'voluntary migration,' a term coined by Malini Bhattacharya, was spoken of by almost all the street vendors and local shop owners whom we interviewed on Parikrama Marg. 'Due to the city's abundance of ashrams and shrines—approximately 4,500—a large number of widows migrate from their villages to Vrindavan,' said Lal Bihari, a rickshaw puller. A few others commented, *'jiska pati nahi hai, uska toh abb bhagwaan hi hai* (the one who has no husband, has only God).' This observation of the local people regarding the widows may not be an accurate one, for what is represented as voluntary migration, may itself be driven by economic forces.

While conversing with a priest whom we met while on Parikrama Marg, we also encountered the utter ignorance and indifference of the local people regarding the pitiful state of these grief-stricken widows. The old Bengali priest outright rejected the fact that Vrindavan is known as the 'City of Widows' and instead, made a strangely outrageous comment, '*Yeh sab behroopiyein hain* (these are master impersonators)'. Or did he mean that their true self is hidden). He held the belief that most women in white were not widows but *Andals* (worshippers of Vishnu). He compared them to the saint, Meera Bai, who dedicated her life to serving the God of Preservation.

Many widows are left with little choice but to reflect on the tragedy of what occurs to them, with religion offering little or no solace. A street widow, who asked to remain anonymous, remarked, 'I came to Vrindavan yearning for my God,' her voice quivering with grief. 'Instead, I've turned into a beggar.' However, one finds that the locals and the widows themselves have a deeply ingrained and internalised attitude of not accepting their deteriorating economic condition as the major factor that determines their survival out of their oppressive marital homes, but rather a belief that faith compelled them to find solace in Vrindavan.

Our interactions with the women who had relocated to Vrindavan in the hope of leading devout lives on the narrow, cluttered streets of Krishna's city showed that many among them had wilfully given up their homes, but were now regretting their actions. Some of them visit their families every year, but despite what Vrindavan offers, they are still glad to return to the city.

As we strolled forward, we came across a long queue in front of the famous Bhajan Ashrams where a lot of women dressed in white were lingering for their daily wages and free meals. The idea behind Bhajan Ashrams is straightforward. These offer modest lodging facilities for travellers and guests visiting Mathura and Vrindavan. Although providing guests with an economical choice, these Bhajan Ashrams also provide financial assistance to one of Vrindavan's largest communities—the widows. Widows who seek to cultivate a spiritual connection with Krishna do so by chanting *bhajans* in these Bhajan Ashrams, where they go once or twice, daily. They see *Kanha* (one of the many names of Lord Krishna) as their spouse and rely on Him to seek redemption or *moksha*. The ashram officials often provide them with a nominal sum of money in exchange for singing *bhajans*.

According to our research, Shri Bhagwan Bhajan Ashram and Maheshwari Kunj Nyas, to name a few, pay the widows a minimum wage of Rs 14 per day, but to our astonishment, the widows seemed fairly content with this meagre financial allowance.

Though acclimatising to the environment of Bhajan Ashrams takes a while, the inhabitants soon become dependent on them and then refuse to try a different way of life. The menial tasks take on a mystical relevance, so much so that when asked to leave this life and get rehabilitation within the family or in an old age home, they often believe that their livelihood is in danger. The widows who consent to this are usually women who are in acute poverty and have seen extreme living conditions. If they are offered an alternate non-religious career, many of them also feel deceived and demeaned. Harbai Amma, an old woman whom we interviewed on our way to Nidhivan, addressed Vrindavan as the 'Land of Charity'. She said that here, one would never go to bed on an empty stomach. Regular *daans* and donations, frequent provisions of *bhandaaras* (free meals) and remittances from foreign visitors evoke a sense of empowerment and self-sustainability in these abandoned women.

However, each widow also had her own tragic story to share. The long queues in front of the Bhajan Ashrams and the frequent altercations among the waiting women made it evident that the supply of *bhajan* singers outstrips the demand. Disappointed and often agitated, a plethora of women had to take to the streets and beg for the days they could not find employment in the Bhajan Ashrams. Most women who were fortunate enough to find some menial jobs at the Bhajan Ashrams felt strangely satisfied with the facilities and assistance provided by the authorities.

The Bhajan Ashram widows are eager to converse and share their experiences. They are welcoming and hospitable towards visitors, even though there is a significant language barrier between the Bengali widows and the locals. A few locals, including the shopkeepers, have managed to learn some Bengali to communicate with this group. The rent in these places is low, so many of these women also reside in the Bhajan Ashrams. In any case, they often choose a location where they need to part with the least amount of money.

We concluded that there are both pros and cons of living in the Bhajan Ashrams and that one must dig deep to unearth the true stories of these widows' lives.

Community as Home

Tale of Harmony Amidst Hardships

| Himanshi Chawla |

© Himanshi Chawla

MANY LOCALS CLAIM that most ashrams in Vrindavan have become an industry, with the widows struggling for sustenance. Some, particularly a sect of pandits, romanticise these widows as 'Meera and *Gopis*' of the modern age, negating their plight. Others show deep empathy for their condition and criticise the society that has outcasted them. However, it is only the widows living in Vrindavan who could tell their story.

On the afternoon of 14 November 2022, a group of widows

was spotted on Parikrama Marg. These widows had found their newly forged metaphorical home, not built out of bricks and cement, but one laid on the foundation of shared experience—of pain, companionship, and the uncertainty of what lies ahead. Most of them hailed from Orissa, West Bengal, Jharkhand and Chhattisgarh. Some had arrived here hearing about widows living in Vrindavan either on TV, while others had been treated as outcasts at home and directed here by society. A few travelled with fellow widows, while others made the journey alone by train. Those who could communicate in Hindi shared their stories with us, students. The underlying thread was that the death of their husbands had left them even more dependent on their families. Their declining health was seen as a further burden, especially when the family had welcomed more capable women to take care of the chores such as their daughters-in-law. Poverty further increased their hardships and made them doubly marginalised.

'We don't sleep starving here', said one of the widows, as the Parikrama Marg's long trail is one of the main attractions for devotees, who regularly distribute *prasad* to the women begging here. Living on the streets, the widows rely on seeking alms outside the temples. Others try to make their living by singing *bhajans*, doing domestic work for local residents or by taking on tailoring tasks among others.

The silver lining for many is the freedom they experience for the first time in their lives. Many street widows choose to continue living on the streets and not in ashrams and home shelters because of this very reason. 'I am free here, happy too that now the husband is not alive to beat me', remarked one widow with a bittersweet laugh. When words failed due to language barriers, it was these shared emotions that bound them together.

The concept of widow pension schemes was foreign to them.

Without bank accounts and lacking support to open one, they faced additional hurdles in accessing these benefits. A 2010 survey conducted by the Guild of Service and supported by UNIFEM revealed that 30 per cent of the widows were unaware of these schemes. Of the 70 per cent who knew, only a quarter received a pension. Only some 18 per cent had applied but did not receive it, while the remaining 58 per cent were unsure whom to approach or how to navigate the process.

These women have been waiting for weeks on the roadside in front of an ashram (which shall remain unnamed), hoping for their turn to receive shelter. They claimed to have registered with their identification documents and are now on the waiting list.

The local shopkeepers on Parikrama Marg have been among the key observers of these happenings. The prevalent corruption of the ashrams was marked by one such eyewitness who runs a shop in front of this ashram. After much hesitation, he recounted an incident involving an elderly widow who approached the ashram for shelter but was asked to donate a miniature gold Krishna shrine in exchange for her board and lodging. She sacrificed all the gold she had on her person, only to be left a destitute when the ashram turned her away.

A rickshaw driver remarked that many ashrams, whether state-owned or trust-funded, are running businesses, with only a few genuinely helping the widows.

Suffering is part of life and no one can escape from it. For these women, it has been inflicted perhaps more than upon others and with widowhood, they are experiencing yet another wave of pain. As Nietzsche said, 'To live is to suffer; to survive is to find some meaning in the suffering.' These women have traded their suffering for freedom and companionship, discovering solace and purpose in each other's company as they navigate their harsh realities.

Beyond the White

A Poem

Himanshi Chawla

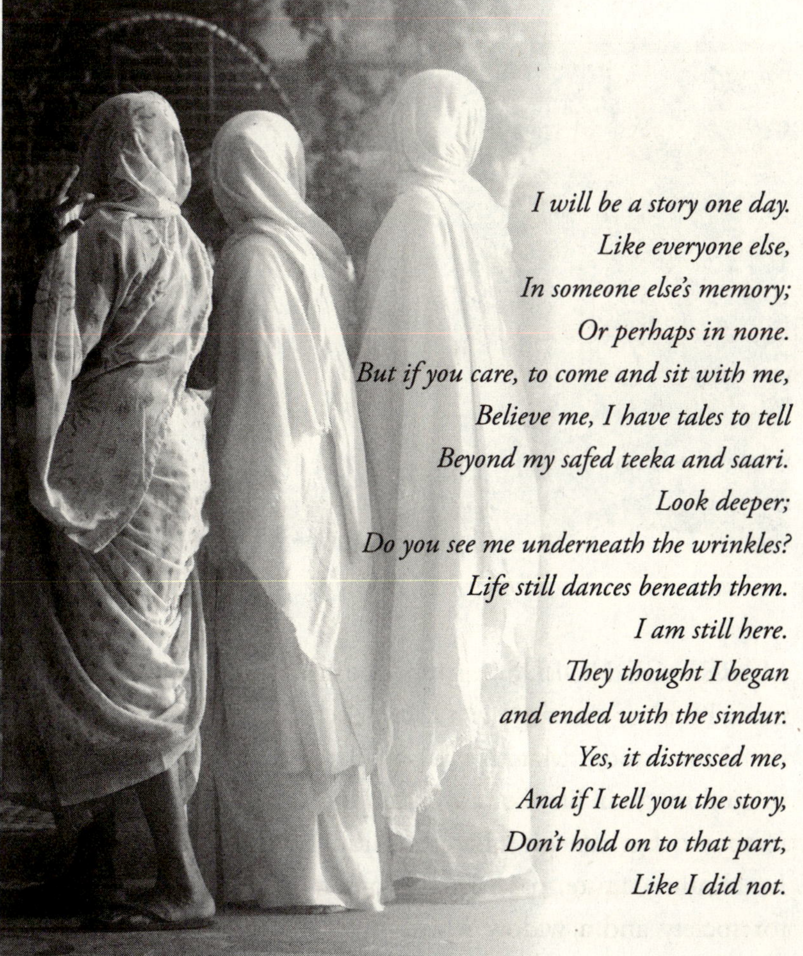

I will be a story one day.
Like everyone else,
In someone else's memory;
Or perhaps in none.
But if you care, to come and sit with me,
Believe me, I have tales to tell
Beyond my safed teeka and saari.
Look deeper;
Do you see me underneath the wrinkles?
Life still dances beneath them.
I am still here.
They thought I began
and ended with the sindur.
Yes, it distressed me,
And if I tell you the story,
Don't hold on to that part,
Like I did not.

Mythological Associations, Local View and Bengali Widows in Vrindavan

| Priya Khandelwal |

Devotees near Nidhivan
© Ananya Aggarwal

MARRIAGE HOLDS A special position in Indian culture. For most Hindus, marriage is a sacrosanct union and an important social institution. Marriage is one of the many *samskaras* one has to go through in life. For a woman, it is the single most important *samskara* that can give her the ultimate fruits of all *samskaras*. In Hindu culture, a married woman is considered auspicious for society and a widow whose husband has died is considered inauspicious and is not accepted by the family and society. Widows all across the country are stigmatised. This can be the reason for widows' migration to the holy city of Vrindavan where they seek shelter in private or in government-run NGOs or decide to settle in the streets of Vrindavan. Often considered a liability on family finances, and to be accepted socially, many widows eventually find themselves in holy places such as Varanasi or Vrindavan.

Vrindavan has approximately 5,000 temples and is the holy place where Lord Krishna spent his childhood. For centuries, it has been a place of refuge for widowed Hindu women.

Reasons for arrival

- For these women, Vrindavan is the land of Krishna and their belief is that Krishna accepts everyone irrespective of their circumstances. They come here to devote their lives to Krishna and to get rid of the miseries by singing *bhajan-kirtans* under the shelter of Krishna.
- They believe Krishna is their life partner. It helps them feel psychologically happy knowing that they have lost their husbands physically, but not spiritually.
- Many widows come to Vrindavan of their own accord, while some escape physically and mentally abusive situations at home.
- Others are simply left and abandoned at Vrindavan by their children or families.
- Some believe in the Karma theory which says that everyone's suffering in this life is the fruit of wrongdoings of their previous life. So, devoting themselves to Krishna, an incarnation of Lord Vishnu, will correct everything and this applies to widows as well. They believe that coming to Vrindavan will ensure them happy, future incarnations.
- The striking contradiction lies in the fact that these widows have devoted themselves to Krishna, but surprisingly they

are not even allowed inside one of the biggest temples of this holy town. Some of them are lucky to live in Ashrams, but others are not, and live in rooms on rent which they somehow manage to pay for from the money they earn through donations and savings. They are living difficult lives here, dependent on charity from the State, NGOs, tourists and the many temples and ashrams of the holy town.

Tale of a widow and Krishna

There are certain mythological stories associated with Hindu widows and their connection with Krishna and Vrindavan. One such mythological story is of Krishna-Arjuna and the widow and her cow. The story goes that once Shree Krishna and Arjuna visited a poor widow who was all alone. She had one cow which was her only means of livelihood. She used to take care of the cow day and night and earned money by selling its milk but at the same time, she was also a devotee of Krishna. Krishna and Arjuna visited her in disguise and were pleased with her gratitude and devotion. Krishna then decided to grant her with a boon that the next day her cow would die so that she could devote herself to Krishna completely and He could grant her a better and more fulfilling incarnation.

Praying to Krishna

Widows as Krishna's wives

A young widow standing in line for Baata Baati ceremony
© Ananya Aggarwal

These widows are called 'Krishna *vadhus*' or 'the wives of Krishna'. The next story is about a demon King Narakasura and the 16,108 wives of Krishna. The demon captured these wives after defeating various Kings. After defeating Narakasura, Krishna is said to have released these women and married them to restore their respect and status at their request. This is how he had an additional 16,000-plus wives. In the same way, Hindu widows ascribe themselves as the wives of Lord Krishna to restore their honour and status which they have otherwise lost in society.

Another story is related to a sixteenth century Bengali social reformer Chaitanya Mahaprabhu who brought a group of widows to Vrindavan to help them escape from the social evil of sati or the fate of immolation. He, along with his disciples, also established some temples at different sites in Vrindavan.

Responses collected from the local population

To learn about the local response to the presence of widows in Vrindavan, we interviewed some shopkeepers and local rickshaw pullers at different sites in the city. The general opinion seems to be that Vrindavan is a safer place for widows who want to devote their lives to Krishna. They maintain that Vrindavan accepts everyone irrespective of their circumstances. The locals have varied perceptions and opinions. Some of them are aware and do agree that a lot of widows come to Vrindavan under duress while some feign ignorance of the fact that Vrindavan is also known for its large population of widows.

Some of the local shopkeepers refused to accept the fact that the place is known for widows: for them, it is the land of Krishna, a sacred land and should only be known for Krishna. Giving the place an identity of the land of widows is something totally unacceptable to them.

A local rickshaw puller gave his own reasons why this place attracts so many widows across the nation. In his own words, '*Vrindavan me koi bhukha nahi marta*'—(None perishes of hunger in Holy Vrindavan, meaning the Lord cares for all). Vrindavan accepts everyone. This place gives them everything, from food to shelter. When we asked him why the widows did not live in ashrams and shelters, he said that they lie and claimed to be shelter-less in order to seek donations from tourists, out of sheer greed.

According to a lady shopkeeper selling toys, these widows migrate to Vrindavan either because they are abandoned and shelter-less or they do not have any source of livelihood, but still, they are happy here. They have created bonds with other widows. She also mentioned that even they, the lady shopkeepers are not allowed inside the temples. This, statement, however, could not be verified.

Woman selling miniature Krishna idols around Prem Mandir
© Ananya Aggarwal

Opinions of foreigners and visitors

When we asked tourists and foreign residents about the presence of the widows, some of them were aware of them, but most had no idea about the Vrindavan widows. However, when those who were unaware were asked to comment if they had seen these women in white, they immediately responded that they had seen a number of ladies in white sarees begging outside temples and in the streets of Vrindavan and had wondered about them.

Widows who come from Bengal

Why do a lot of widows in Vrindavan belong to the Bengali community? What are the reasons behind the huge percentage of Bengali widows in Vrindavan?

- The reasons of course includes the story associated with Chaitanya Mahaprabhu and the reform work and devotion associated with that great saint, as outlined in the story.
- The second reason behind this could emerge from the Bengal Renaissance and indigenous patriarchy whose structure ensured that the Bengali Hindu community isolated the widows as a social category itself rather than just marginalising them as individuals so that they would never reclaim the property and other socio-economic rights and men could establish their control over them.

We sought answers from an old *Mahapujari* from one of the Bhajan Ashrams who was probably in his seventies. He said that the first reason for Bengali widows' immigration to Vrindavan is poverty.

Second, he said that most of the people and Hindu communities in Bengal are non-vegetarians. Despite being brought up on a non-vegetarian diet, after their husband's death, they had to convert to a sparse vegetarian diet, according to social norms. An emphasis on 'a pure and simple' life then brings them there.

The third reason that he gave us was that the men in Bengal remained busy with higher education till quite a late age. Yet they choose to marry girls of comparatively younger age, and the age gap between the partners is quite visible. The men die earlier than their partners and women who get widowed decide to spend the rest of their lives in Vrindavan.

These responses proved to be eye-openers for our team.

Inside the Shelters and Homes

THIS SECTION HAS essays about students' explorations and experiences of widow shelters, both government-owned and those run by NGOs as well as an old age home that houses widows. The Ma Dham Ashram stands out as a model of good practice for its good infrastructure, implementation, active, ongoing research and empathetic policies and programmes. Its success seems to lie in its incorporation of a multi-generational, multipronged approach that promotes sustainability and dignity.

There are also a few narratives here of other homes that highlight the challenges that the widows face, besides the constraints, repression and unhappiness that the inmates experience at some of these homes. Some also experience abuse. The very limited resources offered by the government should also be stepped up for this deprived and unfortunate community.

A Visit to Ma Dham

| Priya Khandelwal and Sakshi Mishra |

VRINDAVAN COMES FROM the word *Vrinda* meaning *tulsi* and *Van,* which means forest. Combining the two words means the forest of *tulsi*.

We began our study from 'Ma Dham', an ashram and shelter home for widows. Ma Dham was founded and is run by the NGO, Guild of Service.

Here every widow is called 'Ma'. In Indian culture, the mother or 'Ma' is accorded the highest status in society, next only to God. The worship of the mother is given unparalleled importance. She is the most glorified and considered worthy of respect and service. Irrespective of their status, and any kind of position in society, widows are treated equally here because 'a mother is a mother always for a child' irrespective of her social and economic status.

This proved to be one of the important places for our research trip. Dr V Mohini Giri was the chairperson and Ms Meera Khanna, is the vice-president of Ma Dham. Currently, it is home to around 55 homeless and destitute women. True to its name, visitors are welcomed by the traditional Hindu culture of performing Aarti and greeted by the Mas who stay here, who chant *Radhe-Radhe* with smiles spread across their faces. In an otherwise noisy city that is always overflowing with pilgrims and devotees, Ma Dham is surprisingly peaceful and calm.

Guild of Service and Ma Dham NGO

It is one of the most important, active and multi-dimensional projects for women's empowerment, providing holistic care and a life of respect and dignity, being run by the Guild of Service. The Guild of Service holds the vision of the protection of human rights for all, especially of those who belong to marginalised groups in society. It is the increasing violations of human rights that inspired the Guild to provide a safe and secure shelter to all those women who are weak, vulnerable, abandoned, and have no one to call their own. The Guild has been involved for nearly four decades in providing services to underprivileged women all over the country.

An old widow/Ma welcoming the team with teeka ceremony at Ma Dham
© Himanshi Chawla

Ma Dham is a home for widows, between the ages of 50 and 108 years. It provides a very pleasant and healthy atmosphere to widowed mothers. Widows, ironically in many sections of our society, are ostracised, victimised and exploited both at mental and physical levels, repeatedly.

Ma Dham provides a home to the widows who were either abandoned or came to Vrindavan of their own will, and is a kind of widow rehabilitation centre in Vrindavan. It is not just a residence for widows, but is truly a happy home.

The premises

The premises include, apart from the rooms for the Mas, a small primary school, an interfaith room, besides rooms for physiotherapy, counselling and OPD. The residents also look after a small organic farm on the premises. It is a safe space for them. The widows are not allowed to do any kind of extensive activities like cooking, cleaning and so on, to avoid taxing them mentally and physically. There is also a Sai temple. There is a story behind this temple—the Sai Murti was abandoned at the gate of the ashram and the ashram inmates adopted it.

At the Vocational Training Centre where they sew bags, *poshaks*, make *donas*, and *batti* to sell and earn their livelihood, some courses are also provided by the Sannidhi Vocational Centre:

1. English speaking classes
2. Computer classes
3. Auxiliary nurses training classes
4. Beauty culture
5. Cutting and tailoring

Ma Dham is an all-inclusive and welcoming place for all religions and communities. It's interfaith room is where different expressions from different religions are painted on the walls. The Mas from different religions come and pray there according to their religious traditions and beliefs.

Ma Dham houses a primary school called Sannidhi Primary School and it teaches students up to class three, who are mostly first-generation learners adopted from six nearby villages recommended by Dr Giri to make the Mas feel happy and fulfilled and also to educate the children. This school caters to two issues: First, it aims to give that love which widows are always seeking to find in their life. Second, it bridges the gap between two generations. The fees is only Rs 100 per month. The organic farm in Ma Dham is the basic source of food for the mothers. Various vegetables are grown there and they have their own *gaushala* (cow shed). In the mess, we could see a weekly menu pasted on the wall which ensured a proper nutritional diet. Another NGO named MCKS Food sends food regularly to Ma Dham. No non-veg is served, because of societal pressure and opposition.

We had a conversation with Anju Chaudhry, the superintendent of the Ma Dham Ashram. She looks after all the Mas, including their medication and hygiene.

We also spoke to Kajal, their counsellor. We saw the OPD, their Interfaith Centre, solar panels, office area and school. The school is open to all the children of the area.

At the small Ma Dham vegetable farm, potatoes, eggplants, carrots, pumpkins, bottle gourds and more is grown. They had eight cows which gave them milk.

First Impressions of Ma Dham

Aditi Chandra, U Sai Sruti, Muskaan,
Sucheta Raj, Ishiqa Shadija, Sakshi Mishra

WE WERE GREETED with smiles and *aarti*. A thin old woman, with a bright smile and a *chandan tilak* on her forehead, welcomed us to Ma Dham. We had not expected such a warm welcome, mainly because of the awareness-raising sessions held before this trip in which the widows were described as living in absolute misery. In contrast, each widow, whom we met at Ma Dham, greeted us with a smile and the traditional Vrindavan pleasing greeting of *Radhe-Radhe*. The widows were poised and inspiring, and although we were greeted with heartwarming smiles, we could detect the sadness and longing in their eyes. We were touched that despite their past trauma, they were greeting us with happy faces. Ms Meera Khanna had earlier commented: 'When they all first come to Ma Dham, they are just people without any kind of personalities. In my opinion, they were like people who were dead from the inside and just bodies mechanically walking and doing things. Why were they like this? Because as a society, we have failed them. We are all accountable for it and not taking that responsibility is the reason why they are like this.'

To reduce their sadness, Ma Dham took this opportunity and built a school. This school solved two problems: First, it gave that love which the widows are trying to find in their lives. Second, working here makes the widows feel useful. The school is till the third grade. Children come mainly from five villages which are adopted by Ma Dham.

An old Ma, who did the teeka ceremony at Ma Dham

We found everyone very fascinating and impressive. But a few widows caught our eye. Let us address the first one as Amma.

Blue Jeans and Shirt wali Amma

Everyone was sitting in the green lawns, sunbathing. Some of them were chatting. This Amma was wearing a blue-coloured shirt and jeans, and she was Bengali.

But she was cool. And her smile was so pretty. She was quite interesting. In a world, where widows wear white sarees, she was wearing jeans and shirt and was smashing every rule of clothing dictated by tradition. She was a rebel with a cause. She even complimented us, telling us that we were all looking gorgeous.

Ramacharitmanas wali Amma and her friend

She was also seated with the other Ammas in the garden area and reading Tulsidas's *Ramcharitmanas* with one of her friends. To our surprise, she told us that she didn't know how to read and write,

Widow/Maa reading *Ramcharitmanas* at Ma Dham
© Ananya Aggarwal

even though she was reading the *Ramcharitmanas*. She was kind enough to read a verse for us in Awadhi language and translated the meaning for us in *Khadi Hindi boli*. She loved it when a number of us clicked pictures of her. And when the whole group sat down to listen to her, every other Amma also wanted the same kind of attention. They needed it. As a group, we tried to communicate with everyone as best as we could.

Amma with the thali

She was the first person in the ashram who greeted us. She was the ashram's mascot in a way, representative of the spirit of the ashram with her positivity. She was a pretty lady in her late sixties or early seventies, and appeared simple and charming in every way. She was smiling the whole time, but her eyes were tinged with sadness. We got the feeling that the lady is a proud survivor of this cruel society. She did the *aarti* gracefully and put *tilak* on everyone's forehead on behalf of the whole ashram.

On speaking to Bina, we learnt that most of them had the freedom to move in and out of the compound during the day and that food and medicines were made available to them daily. The women looked content and peaceful to live in the facility.

Binaji, along with sharing her story in our interview with her, also shed light on how widows in the country do not get the pension that they are legally entitled to receive from the government. She talked about how the widows do not receive adequate financial aid from the government and shed light on how widows are often subjected to bad behaviour by men and rejection by society.

A Few Case Studies at Ma Dham

Harshita Singh, Mansi,
Akshita Sharma, Sakshi Sharma

FORTY-YEAR-OLD Karuna V J was a resident of Mumbai, Maharashtra, and came here with a neighbour voluntarily in 2016. She is a polio patient with 65 per cent impairment and got her education till the ninth standard in Mumbai. When she was around twenty-three years old, she was married off to a man, by her brother. She found that her husband was mentally unfit and used to listen to his mother only. So, Karuna decided to leave him without getting divorced. Her mother-in-law had beaten her once or twice and would threaten her. She is a polio patient and is unable to walk independently, so her friend accompanied her to Vrindavan. She was very happy with her friend in Ma Dham.

She was blaming herself again and again that earlier a good arranged alliance had been proposed for her. The man was handsome and rich and wanted to marry her, but she had refused and later, she was married off to this man who was mentally unfit. She also said that her sister-in-law had come to take her back home, but she declined to go. She received a pension of Rs 1,500 in her bank account. She works as an *aaya* in Sannidhi Primary School in the ashram but gets no wages.

Widows in the garden at Ma Dham
© Ananya Aggarwal

However, her details did not match the report at Ma Dham. She said that she was married, but the document said that she was not. Also, she had said that it was her brother who had got her married, but the document said she did not have a family or any siblings. After her parents died, she lived with her neighbour.

She said she was not paid for her job in school, but the document said she was paid Rs 1,000 monthly.

It seemed she had mental health issues, which would explain the discrepancies.

Although, they get love and all kinds of facilities at the Ma Dham, the yearnings to meet and live with their own blood relations seems to be ever-present among all the inmates.

Another lady we interviewed said that she was denied admission to other shelters when she arrived at Vrindavan, because they felt she was 'too young'. She was relieved to be accepted at Ma Dham and has lived here ever since.

A third Ma said that she used to love dancing and singing

in the past and was traumatised when her husband's brother left her at Ma Dham after she was widowed. He also took away her property and papers.

Another subject described herself as a 'Covid widow.' She said that she came to Vrindavan for peace of mind. She said that she would not like to remarry or have children as children abandoned their parents these days.

The 108-year-old widow was a happy survivor. She stayed at the shelter because she annoyed her family by constantly running out into the streets to beg. She was happier here.

We spoke to many Mas and they all reiterated that widowhood was the worst misfortune. They would not wish it on anyone, and prayed that they never have to face the same situation in their next birth.

A Session with Dr Meera Khanna

Priya Khandelwal, Ayushi Pal, Sakshi Mishra

Dr Meera Khanna
© Ananya Aggarwal

WE HAD AN interactive conversation about the social, cultural, political, economic, and historical factors affecting widows and their lives with one of the key trustees of Ma Dham, Dr Meera Khanna, who is also a writer, poet, gender rights activist, and an eloquent speaker. She is also the executive vice-president of the Guild of Service, which was founded by V Mohini Giri. She spearheaded a global alliance called 'The Last Woman First.' Meera ji is also a co-founder and South Asia chapter chair of Every Woman Coalition. Dr Khanna works in the development sector and focuses on women's empowerment and capacity building, especially in rural India.

We got an insight and better understanding of this deep-rooted issue after talking to Dr Khanna. The session started with her asking about our thoughts on Ma Dham. We then asked her questions.

In her words, it is because of patriarchy that women are suffering so much. But ironically, they are both the survivors as well as the upholders of patriarchy. It is us women who are making our own lives difficult, in some way. Widows believe that they have done something wrong in their lives. She also talked about the internalisation of socio-cultural norms, widowhood in Nigeria and the Brahmanical structure that has been entrenched within society and facilitated the discrimination against widows in India. She described widowhood as an economic crisis and stressed on the need for affirmative action for the widows.

She delved into the cross-caste culture and agreed that the discrimination is more among higher castes than among lower castes. It is because of the availability of resources in the upper caste, that the widows in a Brahminical patriarchal society are pushed to the margins and can be seen as 'physically alive and socially dead'. Brahmins in order to institutionalise this section of women made some codes of conduct for them like wearing white clothes, shaving their heads, and eating *sattvik bhojan* and so on. Women are being doubly traumatised, first when they are controlled by the males in their lives, and second, when they are made to obey the norms of society.

The place of women in Indian society is equal to that of the Shudras in the *varna* system of yore. Both were secluded and restricted from performing certain jobs. Shudras can't do certain kinds of jobs and women are restricted to roles such as being child bearers and family caretakers.

The guilt of being the cause of widowhood surrounds a lot of widows in Vrindavan. Dr Khanna also threw light upon how a lot of blessings that are given to women reinforce sexist roles. She also spoke about the caste culture relating to widows. The higher caste people are more conscious about their values and respect, and the widows are made to suffer more because of it. Remarriage of widows is usually promoted in a lower caste setting because they need more labour, but not among upper castes.

Widows outside live with societal pressure, but in shelter homes or ashrams, there is no societal pressure and that is why they are free. Here widowhood ceases to be delimiting because of lack of reinforcement. She focused on three factors:

- Patriarchy
- Patrilineal Inheritance
- Patri-locality

Patriarchy : Refers to protection of male members. With time, this concept came from pastoral to agrarian communities wherein the protector becomes superior because of physical abilities and the protected becomes the inferior. Widow discrimination is maximum in Hindu communities. Among Brahmins, women have two life goals: Reproduction responsibility and being part of religious rituals with men to ensure their salvation. Without a man in their life, they have no purpose and hence the household thinks there is no need for their physical and social presence. They are thus, abandoned.

Patrilineal Inheritance: In earlier times, women were devoid of their share in property from both sides, but now it is illegal to deny them their share, through amendments made to the Hindu Succession Act. Now, women can assert a right to their husband's inheritance. But, they are hesitant to assert their rights as they fear that by doing so, they will jeopardise their good relations with their in-laws. Thus grooms are chosen from an outside village so that women can get detached from their maternal homes.

Under patrilineal inheritance, she spoke about the Sharda Act, property rights and the Hindu Succession Act. In Rig Veda, there was no discrimination against widows. They were given equal rights and respect. With the Aryans invasion, society became aggressive and women's honour was under threat, and thus, they needed physical protection. Patriarchy flourished.

Patrilocality: It is the system whereby a woman lives at her husband's home after marriage.

Dr Khanna also discussed how we can never escape the repercussions of the caste system in India and how we women are survivors of patriarchy, but at the same time, also uphold it. It is us women who are making our own life difficult in some ways.

She added that many of the women came here voluntarily as they were fed up with their families and their misbehaviour towards them. Some came here to achieve *Vanaprastha Ashrama*, to attain salvation as mentioned in the old, religious texts. Most of them, however, found themselves abandoned, and so ended up here. Many of them are now getting and enjoying freedom in their lives here.

She described the much-practised system of *Baata-baati* where widows get donations from visitors and gurus. But even that has become like a business here. People donate what they want to, like blankets, sarees, and *ladoos* and not what these women and the Ashrams really need like medicines, adult diapers, walkers and other such things. Widows, however, collect the donated items, even what they don't need, then sell them and make money.

Widows are not always aged. They are just not being taken care of by their own families and are abandoned here. We need to have female-headed households to eradicate poverty, social evils, and crimes. To progress and prosper, women must contribute to the GDP of the country.

We asked her why there were still so many street widows even though there seemed plenty of shelter homes for them in Vrindavan. She replied that it was primarily because all of them don't want to live in ashrams because this is the first time that they are experiencing freedom and they naturally compare this to the patriarchal households, in which they hitherto lived and where they were not given any freedom at all. Moreover, there are certain rules in ashrams that they have to abide by.

She concluded the session by alerting us to the subject of widowhood and reiterated that it should be discussed on a much wider scale, so that the myths surrounding widows and how they survive are busted.

This interaction with Dr Khanna left us wondering about the condition of widows outside this ashram, in Vrindavan and beyond.

An Interview at AIWC Old Age Home

Muskan Dhankher, Aditi Chandra, U Sai Sruti, Sucheta Raj, Ishiqa Shadija

Team interviewing the locals at Rangnath ji Mandir
© Ishiqa Shadija

This old-age facility is run by the All India Women's Conference (AIWC) and also takes care of widows. The shelter is in poor condition and offers negligible facilities with its small rooms packed with senior women. Here we interacted with several widows, observed their condition, and took down notes. The home, itself, was in poor condition with little to no maintenance of the rooms, with the widows cramped into a small unhygienic space in locked, windowless rooms. There was not enough space to accommodate them all and their rooms were locked with a *mota taala* and they were not allowed by the warden to go out on their own. We, however, managed to do a series of interviews with these women. A few of the widows we interacted with pointed out that the current warden does not let them go out and medicines are also denied to them. This did not happen before.

As most widows were from Bengal, we needed a person to translate for us. But the odd thing was that the translator tried to drown their narrative, spoke over them and seemed to negate their experiences. We instinctively noted the discrepancy between what the widows wished to share and what the translator wanted to censor out.

The incident gave us an insight into the extent to which the widows' narratives are silenced and how the true condition of such shelters is never revealed to outsiders, researchers and those documenting their condition.

Konaklata Audhikari

She is now a senior lady who got married when she was just eleven and became a widow at eighteen. Her husband was forty-five and died of alcoholism. She has been living in Vrindavan for twenty-five years. She can barely walk as she suffers from acute arthritis and yet I saw this spirited eighty-eight-year-old do every little chore on her own.

Family Background

- She was married at an early age, and has no children, or property.
- She sold some land after the death of her husband and started living with her sister and brother-in-law. But after their death, she came to Vrindavan and has

been living here ever since.

- She seemed very sensitive, and was approached accordingly.
- When we asked her what change she wished to see, she simply said that she just wanted her sufferings to end and was waiting for her death here in the land of Krishna.

Naulita Dasi

Thin with grey hair, seventy-five-year old Naulita wore a pale yellow saree which was once white. She was married at twelve and widowed at twenty-eight. She repeats a story that could belong to many of the widows here: rickshaw-puller father, nine siblings, seven girls and two boys. She was the eldest, and was married off to an old man.

Sumitra

Sumitra is sixty years old. She came to Vrindavan six months ago from Nainital. Her sister left her here. Since then, she had not gone back to her home. Her husband married thrice so she left the house after she had had enough of the 'humiliation'.

Menka Mondal

Menka Mondal is eighty-two. She came to Vrindavan, twelve years ago from Asansol, West Bengal. She was married at sixteen years of age and widowed at twenty-one. Her husband died of diarrhoea. She willingly gave away all her possessions, including the house of her husband to family members.

All these women did not receive any pension from the government, and make do with just their nominal, Sulabh pension.

A widow standing in lIne for Baata Baati
© Himanshi Chawla

A Visit to Maitreyi Ashram

Smriti Ahuja

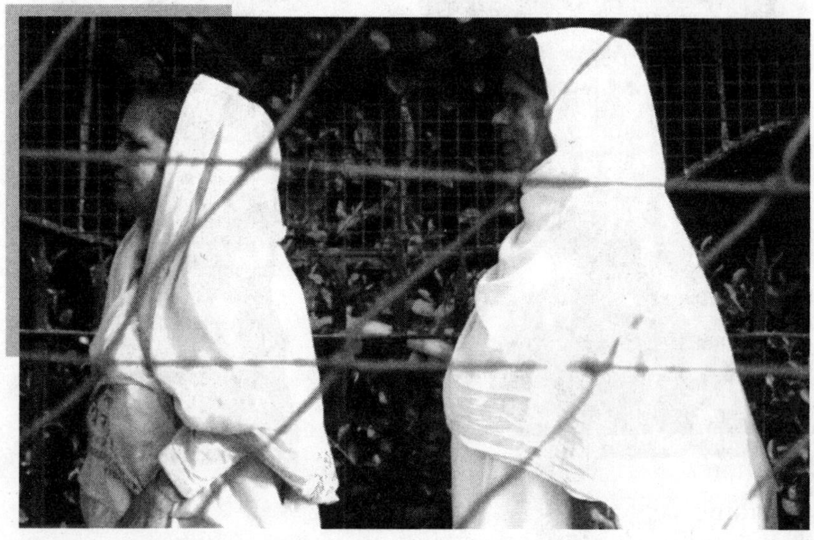

In the bustling city of Vrindavan, there lies a small widow ashram away from the noise and colours of the city. Maitreyi Ashram attempts to create a better life for widowed women who were either forced to leave their homes or felt like they had no other choice. Some even stated that they came to Vrindavan and Maitreyi for religious purposes and to be close to Krishna. Overall, the reason for each of the widow's presence in the ashram was different but for most, it followed a common pattern of discrimination, abuse and undertones of patriarchy.

For our team, who went to Maitreyi, the first thing that we observed was the long distance that was covered from Maa Dham, which is located close to multiple prime locations in Vrindavan. It was an almost hour-long journey via the prime means of transportation in Vrindavan, an e-rickshaw. The ashram was fairly isolated and completely cut off from the lively parts of the city.

When our team arrived at Maitreyi, we noticed that the ashram was undergoing a renovation. We were asked to wait as they called all the widow residents to meet us outside the building. Despite our insistence to go inside and look at the residential facilities, the kitchen and more, we were stopped from doing so. The reason for this is still not clear to us. On the other hand, the women warmly welcomed our team and seemed happy at the thought of conversing with us. Each member approached different groups of women and tried to be as cordial with the interview process as possible. Firstly, our team made sure that the consent forms were explained and willingly signed by these women. Further, we sought permission to record them. Our findings and observations were interesting. The diversity of this group of women was more in terms of the regions where they are from than their age. Most of them were over fifty.

When trying to understand the history and background of these women, two primary patterns emerged. Most of the women had come to Maitreyi out of sheer necessity. Their life at their 'home' required them to move away. Multiple forms of situations led to this conclusion. Either their children did not want them at home because of how widows are treated or because of pre-existing conflicts. Whatever the reason, they believed they had to leave as it was the only right way for a widowed woman to live. But they still justified their children's decision.

The second pattern consisted of women who came on their own because they had no family members to turn to. After the death of their husbands, some of them worked on their own and lived alone for multiple years whilst also experiencing traumatic experiences like the death of their children, fraud and abuse. But after many years, when it became physically difficult to continue with labour of this form, they came to Vrindavan to live out the rest of their days in peace and near God.

Being at the ashram gave these women a sense of security, even though restrictions imposed by the owner and manager pained their hearts. Some of these women clearly stated that they were not allowed to wear bright and colourful clothes and were also forbidden from wearing jewellery such as bangles and earrings. Those who used to apply sandalwood/*chandan* were also not allowed to do so. There was also a strong insistence on making these women wear white to keep up with traditions. They found it unfair because, despite the restrictions that widowhood in general imposed upon them, they wished to adorn themselves with whatever ornaments they possessed. They stated how they were ordered to live in a simple way, without indulgences, the same way in which the ashram was located away from the colours of the city. This performance of widowhood might have been implemented with the aim to receive more donations.

These women, however, lack support and encouragement from the organisation. Moreover, these women do not go out much. It's also perhaps because the ashram is too far away from most places and temples.

Another conflicting and saddening thing that we noted was the image of the manager as painted by the interviewees. A contrast was observed as in we noticed that almost all Bengali widowed women favoured the manager, and believed him to be their true caretaker and gave the same positive answers no matter what the question was. However, the others who were from other regions claimed that the manager was biased in his treatment and favoured the Bengali women. They insisted that the women from West Bengal were treated better as opposed to those from other regions.

This bias was also observed in a talk we had with Subhadra who talked in detail about the hardships she had faced in life before coming to Maitreyi. She described her husband's death, working and living alone, being cheated of more than Rs 50,000 and about how she had fallen sick and spent half a month in a government hospital.

With all these troubles, she had finally decided to come to Vrindavan. But when asked about her life in the present and if she was happy, she visibly gulped before answering this question and adopted an even more sorrowful tone than before. Her earlier hope for a better life in Vrindavan had been long crushed. She stated that the manager was unfair towards her and continuously told her to leave the ashram. But where could she go?

This conversation, sadly, was not extended past this point. The manager overheard the conversation and was visibly unhappy with what was being discussed. He asked us to stop recording even though we had asked the interviewees for their consent beforehand. He said that we were wrong to ask these questions and abruptly ended our visit. We had to wrap up quickly. Later, he called some of us to his office where he proceeded to lecture our team on our *sanskaras* and how research is supposed to be conducted, and that we should only have asked about their past and not their present. He even suggested that this research should have been conducted from the comfort of our homes. The members were further asked about their family histories and how our *sanskaras* should hold more value than a research project. Following this, we made our way back, drained and disappointed.

But the impact of widowhood is not limited to what happens within an ashram. It is equally important to note the pain inflicted by government inattention. Gayatri Mukherjee said in her interview that she only received Rs 200 to Rs 300 every month as a pension and wished the government would increase the amount to at least Rs 1,000. The government, at their end, and other NGO-based organisations need to work better to truly help and improve the living conditions of these women who are not only subjected to family-inflicted isolation but are also vulnerable to societal isolation, exploitation and abuse.

Maitreyi sadly represents the condition of widowed women in most ashrams in India. Underfunded care, power in the wrong hands and a lack of awareness among widowed women are some of the reasons behind the current, unfortunate situation of these women.

- Need for reform is evident. Pensions should increase and be universally given.
- There should be a fixed widow compensation and not be based on a quota system.
- The compensation should be based on the current living cost.
- Management of these NGO-run ashrams should be fair and just.

Perceptions Across Spaces

THIS SECTION LOOKS at the results of a survey conducted at the Janki Devi College, in New Delhi to garner perceptions about widowhood and its representations in contemporary media. It also brings together impressions registered during a temple visit and an overview of what Bhajan Ashrams offer widows in Vrindavan.

Women's safety, their identity outside of marriage, their negotiation of widowhood in these fast changing times, their financial security and the struggle for survival remains abiding concerns in present times.

Financial Condition of Widows in Vrindavan and the Concept of Bhajan Ashrams

Megha Saini, Diksha Sharma, Nikita Yadav, Nitakshi, Muskaan Jain

QUITE A FEW widows in Vrindavan have been residing there for more than 70 years, and they have figured out a way of life that is suitable for them. According to our research in the field, we found that most of the widows are from Bengal. The most likely reason for this could be the inheritance law in West Bengal, where a widow has the right to the property of her husband. And so it led to a culture in Bengal to abandon women from the household after their husbands die to prevent them from claiming the property. Usually the children of the widow, mainly the son and daughter-in-law are involved in this practice of abandoning the old mothers in the streets of Vrindavan.

A number of these women rely on nominal daily earning or on *daan* or charity. For some, Bhajan Ashrams play a vital role in providing them with basic pay for them to get through their days, while others just roam the streets trying to get enough money for their daily meals. These street widows either beg or do minor jobs, like putting a *teeka* on a tourist's forehead, in order to get a nominal amount from them. It is very interesting to observe them doing this job as they almost climb over tourists or sometimes forcefully anoint them with the *teeka*. In return, people have to give them some money. The pay from a Bhajan Ashram or what they earn on the streets is not nearly enough, but they somehow manage to survive.

In Vrindavan, the team spoke to a local resident, a boatman. He runs a boat ride business on the Yamuna Ghat for many years, a business he inherited from his forefathers. He said that 'in Vrindavan it is not a difficult task for anyone to survive.' He described it as a tourist place where people come in the spirit of Krishna *bhakti*, and do a lot of *daan* (charity) in the name of *dharma*. One could get enough food for the day simply by sitting outside any temple.

The widows receive a lot of donations daily from locals, tourists, Bhajan Ashrams, and the Government. One such example is of the *Baata-Baati* ceremony, in which all the widows of Vrindavan are invited and are given loads of donations. However, a lot of these women end up selling whatever donations they get for extra cash. This shows that these women are adept at generating income in an innovative fashion. Most of these women do not have a bank account. They rely on cash and spend whatever they earn in a short period of time.

Bhajan Ashrams

The concept of Bhajan Ashrams is simple. These are hotels/ guesthouse-like structures where rooms are available for pilgrims visiting Vrindavan. Apart from guest rooms, the building has large halls for the widows to sing Krishna *bhajans* or perform other religious tasks that only a widow is supposed to do. These affordable options for visitors also offer financial support to widows, one of the biggest communities of the vulnerable in Vrindavan.

Shri Bhajan Ashram
© Ananya Aggarwal

Bhajan Ashrams are establishments where widows visit once or twice a day to sing *bhajans* in order to spiritually connect with Krishna. Many of them believe that after their husband's death, they must devote their life to the Lord. They consider Krishna as their husband and trust Him to give them an easy and respectful life. In Indian culture, husbands are obliged to support their wives financially, to keep them secure, and therefore, these widows seek that safety from the divine god. In return for singing *bhajans*, they are offered a small amount of money daily by the ashram authorities. This monetary prize can also be seen as a bait for them to keep involved in spirituality, and not get into any unethical practice for survival. This encourages the display of devotion in their daily lives.

Shri Bhagwan Bhajan Ashram

This is one of the major Bhajan Ashrams in Vrindavan which is associated with the Fogla Ashram. Fogla Ashram is near the ISKCON temple in Vrindavan. This Bhajan Ashram is in Goda Vihar, near Ranganath Temple in Vrindavan. In the market area, we met a Bengali widow, who led us to the Bhajan Ashram. Her language was not very familiar, but we were able to understand a few words, and inferred that she lived nearby, but chose not to go to the Bhajan Ashram.

Her appearance indicated that she was not the typical, vulnerable widow we would expect at a place like Vrindavan. Rather, she seemed headstrong and confident. She showed us the way inside the bhajan ashram, a private establishment that is also known as 'Vidhwa Ashram'.

Observing the environment inside, we noticed that almost all the widows present there were Bengali. When we walked in, a religious satsang was on. An old lady, herself a widow, was conducting the session in Bangla. There were rooms on all four sides of the building for the pilgrims and a large hall which is seemingly dedicated to widows only.

There was space for about 700-800 people in these halls and it was filled with Bengali widows only, but some were from Uttar Pradesh and Madhya Pradesh, too. All of them were old, between fifty to ninety years of age. They all seemed immersed in Krishna *bhajans*. All of them were clad in cotton sarees of light colours, but few were also in red and other coloured sarees, exploding the myth that widows should only be seen in white. And of course, none of them wear makeup or jewellery. They displayed a low energy level and did not seem enthusiastic to even enjoy the rhythm of the *bhajans*.

As we went inside, a lady pointed to the room where the administrators were to be found. The administrators asked us to take permission from the owner before talking to the widows. They did not allow us to interview any of the widows or click photographs. Moreover, none of the administrators were willing to talk to us in the absence of their manager.

Whatever we learnt was from the authorities, nothing at all from the widows.

The ashram opens at 6 am and closes at 7 pm. During these hours, multiple widows visit and spend their time in the premises singing *bhajans* and practising spirituality. They leave the ashram as soon as the clock strikes 7 pm. The widows earn Rs14 for every day they visit the Bhajan Ashram to sing bhajans. The ashram also provides one meal of the day to the widows in addition to all the donations like sarees, blankets, medicines provided on an occasional basis. Local people and tourists frequently donate supplies to the Bhajan Ashrams.

An old guard, near one of these ashrams, who was in his sixties, had become a great source of information for us. He politely answered all the questions we asked him. Young widows also visited the ashram often, usually in the early morning hours. The Ashram's *maalik* lives in Delhi and usually takes care of the financial aspect. The Bhajan Ashram also brings out a magazine related to spirituality and Krishna. Sometimes it focuses on the widows that come to the ashram to sing and pray.

Maheshwari Kunj Nyas

That old guard from Shri Bhagwan Bhajan ashram guided us to the nearby Maheshwari Kunj Nyas. This was comparatively smaller, but built more recently, so it was more modern. The Shri Bhagwan Bhajan Ashram closes at 7 pm, so some of the widows head towards the Maheshwari Kunj in order to make extra money. This ashram has comparatively less space for widows and has a slightly different way of working. This ashram opens at 6:30 am and closes at 8:30 pm and is noticeably cleaner than the Bhajan Ashram. The manager here also spoke more freely to us. There are a lot of donations being made towards the widows by the locals and by the ashram authorities. The widows are paid Rs14 per day on a 10-day basis.

The widows usually seem uninterested in talking to people during their *bhajan* timings, as they prioritise spirituality and the little money they make from it. One woman, however, was intrigued by the team and initiated a conversation, herself. Upon further interaction, some disturbing facts emerged. The woman was dressed with *sindoor* and *bindi* and claimed that although she was not a widow, she had been living in Vrindavan for the past ten years. She explained that she was unhappy in her marital house and had made the decision to leave when both her boys married. She revealed that although she still spends a few days at her hometown in Jharkhand, every year, she hasn't been to her marital house in ten years. She revealed her tragic tale when questioned about how she was living as a widow yet wearing the *sindoor* and *bindi*, symbols of a married woman. She did this because she felt secure in wearing them and was sure that no man would intentionally hurt a married woman. Otherwise, men would think she was alone and had no protector if she did not wear the *sindoor*. Moreover, she was apprehensive of being molested. It is distressing to note that a woman who wished to have no ties with her husband still needed to wear the evidence of his existence merely to be safe. This says a lot about women's security in Indian cities. She still feels the need to assume the identity of a married woman even after ten years of leaving her marital home.

Most of the women at these Bhajan Ashrams are keen to talk and share their stories. They are friendly and intrigued about a new presence at the premises. Most of them are from Bengal so there exists a huge language barrier between the widows and the local people. A few local people, such as shopkeepers, have learnt a bit of Bangla to be able to interact with this community.

Many of these women live in the Bhajan Ashrams, as the rent here is less. They generally choose among the options where they have to spend the minimum for rent and living expenses.

The women live simple lives, earning and spending on a daily basis. They wear simple sarees, usually white or of light colours. Although they do not know Hindi, they are extremely polite and manage to comprehend what we said and were able to conduct an everyday, workable conversation in Hindi.

Interviews of Foreign Tourists and Devotees at ISKCON Temple

Smriti Ahuja, Prerna, Samriddhi Pendharkar, Anchal Sethi

AMIDST THE HUSTLE and bustle of devotees and preachers at the busy temple, the diverse interactions with foreign devotees and local visitors allowed our team to take a look at Hinduism, human nature and the complete ignorance prevailing in religious spaces. The foreign devotees choose to be immersed in the spiritual aspect that Vrindavan has to offer, rather than familiarising themselves with the social, cultural and regional reality of the place. They are selectively following the religion and spiritual practices of ISKCON which brings them peace and have learnt to ignore the deeply layered practices of casteism and undertones of patriarchy that the same Hindu religion is also coloured with. Widows are not seen around

ISKCON Temple
© Ananya Aggarwal

the ISKCON Temple, and one wonders why widows do not go there. Are they not allowed to enter the temple?

First, we interviewed a spiritual preacher. Formerly an engineer, the preacher regularly telecast live sessions on a spiritual television channel. He claimed that education pulled him to the dark side of humanity. It was because of this kind of lifestyle, that he was now able to see the bright side of life and humanity. He was a firm believer in karma and believed, like most of the people at ISKCON, that the plight of widows in Vrindavan or anywhere in India was unfortunate but then went ahead to justify the existence of the widows, their mistreatment and existence of such practices. According to him, the widows were paying back for the misdeeds of their past lives.

The preacher, too, had a patriarchal mindset and did not want his ideas on widows and widowhood to be questioned. Despite knowing that widowhood is a stage, a lot of women have to pass through, most people connect and justify their ill-treatment with karma. He also told us how ISKCON provides support to widows of different villages by conducting activities like meditation. According to him, only meditation could erase the bad karma and make the current life of widows better. The preacher recommended several books for us to read. The conversation had initially focused on how education and books are corrupting the minds of today's youth, but when he mentioned books that supported patriarchy and his spiritual values, he seemed to contradict himself. Here was an educated, seemingly spiritual person who should be helping others to bring about change, but was advocating the opposite. He never directly answered any of the questions we asked him, deftly sidestepping them every time by saying 'It's the price they are paying for the misdeeds of their past life.'

Similar to the preacher, we interviewed a Krishna devotee from Slovenia. He preferred being called by his spiritual name, Mahaprabhugaura Das. He had visited Vrindavan seventeen times in his devotion towards Krishna and firmly believed that following Krishna and his ideologies had provided him with the answers to life. The devotee also provided us with an insight into the ISKCON temple and the followers of Lord Krishna in Slovenia. Das was aware of Vrindavan being called the 'City of Widows' and also blamed women's bad karma for the struggles that they were facing as widows. He even claimed that women who lose their husbands often act as victims to seek attention and money.

He stated that the colour white is superior to every colour. He ended the interview with similar thoughts as that of the preacher, that is, only the widowed women's good deeds can lead to a better next life.

An American visitor had similar perceptions about karma. Originally from Moldova, which lies close to Ukraine, Yugaha Priti had come on a pilgrimage with her guru, Romapada Swami. She came across Krishna Consciousness after coming to America and had eventually become a firm believer. Her belief was that surrendering to the Lord will bring about rational thinking and free us from corruption under the guidance of the 'Brahmanas' or (Vedic teachings), affirming that these scriptures could never give wrong guidance. As stated by the interviewees, they believed that karma from one's previous life dictates their present life. We talked to her about her perspective. She believed that if an individual is spiritually elevated, such as being a Krishna devotee and being well-versed with the Vedas, then such a person would not suffer from hardships of life as Krishna will protect them. While she agreed with us that the condition of widowed women was saddening and unfortunate, she was also unable to take a stand against her beliefs which justified the treatment of widows, ultimately leaving her confused.

She said she was not against widow remarriage, but added that that if one were to devote oneself to Krishna fully, it would nullify her individuality so much so that a widow would not need to remarry. Her insistence was repetitive as if to instil the same sense within us while trying to free herself of her confusion.

Last, we met a new devotee from Kenya, who identifies himself by his spiritual name, Mana-Siksha. Having only arrived a month ago, he serves at the temple. His views were clearly ambiguous, seeing he had come to Vrindavan solely on hearsay, and was unaware that Vrindavan is also called the 'City of Widows'. He grew curious and asked our opinions on the state of Indian women and the patriarchal structure that plagues our society. We asked him how Krishna Consciousness taught disciples to treat women, and he believed that in the age of Kalyug, it is difficult to maintain a set of values, and so the only protection we can provide women, is education. But he was unaware that young girls are often deprived of even this basic protection in India.

The heavy indoctrination of ISKCON was underlined in each interview, and how the concept of karma was iterated to justify the hardships of widowhood. Our interviews brought up examples of the legitimisation of inequality and injustice by using a partial understanding of religion: a fix to your problems while carefully hiding the casteist and patriarchal aspect of the same system.

Representation of Widows in Indian Cinema

| Samriddhi Pendharkar |

THIS ESSAY LOOKS at the general perceptions of the twenty-first century youth living in metropolitan cities whose general understanding of widows either comes from stories they have heard from their elders or through media representations on the subject, usually a secondhand source. Their perceptions do not come from talking to the sorry-looking, lonely, all-white saree clad women of Vrindavan, but rather by seeing them represented in popular media. It is not that their perceptions are entirely untrue. In some conservative families, widows are indeed considered bad luck and shunned, and women, especially those who are old and illiterate, and not capable of sustaining themselves, indeed travel from afar to cities like Vrindavan to find peace. But here too, they end up on the streets, begging at the steps of temples. However, one seldom finds them inside the 'holy structures' owing to the stereotypes and degradation of their image through popular and baseless narratives based on bad luck. Widows are rarely mentioned in the literature on poverty, in public debates on social policy, or even by the women's movement. While the media does not use a helpless widow as one of its necessary stock characters, it has, in a sense, taken the character out of the narrative entirely. However, the older representations can still be seen in some daily soaps. Interestingly, movies and web series feature a socially unaccepted and more empowered transgressive role of the widow.

Our entry point

We circulated a Google form for youngsters (between the ages 18-25) to some students at Janki Devi Memorial College, University of Delhi. The students were asked to write their perceptions on three major questions, to which 80 responses were received in total.

- What is the first thing that comes to the minds of young people when they come across the word 'widow'?
- Myths they have heard of or believe in, regarding widows.
- How are widows represented in Indian Cinema?

The responses collected generally showed a pattern of similar answers. While a lot of responses included the literal meaning of the term, many did convey the impression that the word 'widow' creates in the minds of the survey group. Out of the eighty responses that were collected, seventy-two included terms like pain, unhappiness, and loneliness. Even in the twenty-first century, amidst the fourth wave of feminism, most youngsters that we questioned brought up an image that seems to correspond to the stereotypical representation of widows.

Though, we do not get to see a lot of widows in white sarees in cities like Delhi, the responses included images of a woman in a white saree. From the responses, we gathered that it is not as if these youngsters believe in the myths and superstitions regarding widows, but rather, they have ingrained the image through their surroundings and through media representations. Most of them have grown up seeing their grandparents and have been exposed to the times in which their elders have lived, through stories and anecdotes.

Widows standing in line for Baata Baati ceremony
© **Himanshi Chawla**

It is believed that, even the food prepared or touched by widows must not be consumed since they are commonly associated with black magic. The image of a lonely, unhappy woman who turns evil and performs black magic and witchcraft and brings evil into the lives of others is still prevalent. Hypothetically, even if a widow turns bitter or negative, it could be as a coping mechanism with the atrocities she has been through at the hands of the same patriarchal society that treats her like an outcast. In our society, sexual agency for a woman, more so for a widow, is out of the question. While a married woman is supposedly a walking womb, a widow is denied any sexual expression.

According to the collected responses, almost all talked about them being harbingers of bad luck. A few mentioned that widows are quite often believed to be responsible for having brought about the demise of their husbands. Mohini Giri had said that 'widows are still accused of being responsible for their husband's death, and they are expected to have a spiritual life with many restrictions which affects them both physically and psychologically.'

Their misery and sufferings are justified as atonements for their karma in a past life. Since they are already regarded unlucky for others and are not supposed to have any kind of sexual or emotional desires, the idea of remarriage is seen as a blot on the family. 'On the one hand, women are venerated as goddesses and considered as the source of the creative feminine power that holds the authority to construct or destroy the universe. On the other hand, they are labelled as evil, an entrance to hell and a bad influence which should be stayed away from.'[1]

The responses included how they are required and expected to live the rest of their life in solitude, minimising their expressions of enjoyment or happiness and staying away from social interaction. They are restricted from auspicious ceremonies to prevent bad luck and jinxing of happiness. Even onions, garlic and spicy or nonvegetarian food are not served to them as these foodstuffs might instigate their sexual desires. The only socially accepted feeling that can be expressed by a widow, therefore, is grief. Young or old, widows give up their vibrant saris, part with their jewellery, and sometimes even shave their hair if they are from more conservative Hindu families. All of this is designed so as not to encourage male sexual desire, according to Dr Meera Khanna, who heads the Guild of Service and is a trustee of the New Delhi-based Women's Initiative for Peace in South Asia, and has contributed articles to *Living Death: Trauma of Widowhood in India.* 'The widow is 'uglified' to deprive her of the core of her femininity,' writes Khanna. 'It is an act symbolic of castration. She is deprived of the red dot between her eyebrows that proclaims her sexual energy.'

In the last question about the media representation of widows, we saw a mix of answers. While some talked about times when we had white saree representation in Indian cinema, others stated recent shifts to a more positive representation. These positive responses speak of how the trajectory of cinema has moved from a time when widows represented in Indian cinema promoted the stereotypical image of white saree-clad, lonely, helpless women to recent representations in Indian cinema. Some other respondents talked about the recent shift from the sad, lonely widow to more ambitious, powerful, and expressive roles. Anything that is represented is always influenced by the ideological preferences of the society of a certain time, and the representation of anything is therefore never in a vacuum. However, it is not only society that forms the literature and media of a place, but it is this that, in turn, moulds the ideologies and opinions of a society, deliberately.

Movies like *Kati Patang, Sholay*, and *Prem Rog* were repeatedly mentioned in the responses we received. In the seventies Bollywood movies, widows are shown as emotionless beings who don't have any desires and do not participate in decision-making for their families.

'Who will marry a widow? It is a sin. We are leading the life of renunciation and also die for the same,' says a character in the 2005 film, *Water*. Here is an archetypal image of a widow. The ideal image of a widow contradicts the fulfilment of love because love's desire is intimacy and passion which is forbidden to a widow. A widow is supposed to live the life of self-renunciation says author Kanwaljit Kaur.

In the seventies movies, widows were treated as outcasts, marginalised and undeserving of any respect. They are shown as vulnerable and requiring male support to sustain and protect them. The vulnerable image is promoted by showing how without a husband the widows are susceptible to harassment. All the talk around is of how the virtue of these silent ones is to be protected because they are seen as helpless women who could be 'influenced' by another male. This is also something that we usually come across in the typical Bollywood representation of widows of the mid and late twentieth century along with the notion that they are financially dependent on males in one way or the other. The power hierarchy shifts from the husband to the son and always the male is the powerful one.

In contrast to this, recent movies like *Pagglait* have created a conscious effort in depicting an ambitious young widow who, in defiance of social expectations, does not shed tears and focuses on empowering herself. Another example is from the web series *Made in Heaven* where remarriage of a mature, educated widow with the mature man of her choice is promoted. Fighting expectations of society and her grown up children who are against the marriage, this widow takes a step forward, and the episode is an appropriate description of how widows are expected to be desireless and unemotional when they are not. Although the series has received appreciation for being one of the few feminist masterpieces to venture out of Indian media, we also need to take into account the fact that the acceptance of this particular episode was probably due to it being available on an OTT platform. Had it been a plot for a movie that receives a more generationally variable and larger audience, this would not have been seen in the same light and with the same acceptance and encouragement.

Conclusion

In our society, marriage is accepted as an important institution. Whether or not a girl wants to get married, her parents will always bring up the idea of marriage as something inevitable, and this is something that most young women in today's India have experienced. Marriage is not just an alliance of a male and female, but of their families as well. Since, the woman is the one who will carry the family lineage forward, she represents the honour of the family. An honour, that at no cost must be tarnished. Thus, a woman is labelled as *manhoos* or a harbinger of bad luck, when she loses her husband. Since society has patriarchal foundations, it, therefore, puts all the burden of family honour on the women of the house. All the reputation of the two families is thus carried by her and the consequences of any mishap are to be faced by her and her, alone. This idea is internalised so deep within the roots of the Indian community that people fail to realise the extent of the internalisation. The stereotypes living in the subconscious of the youth, that were accepted without questions while listening to their families or watching cinema of earlier decades, surfaced in their consciousness while responding to the survey, perhaps. The patriarchal hegemony created in the families at the root level, is what leads to the internalisation of such ideas.

Afterword

Swati Pal
Professor and Principal,
Janki Devi Memorial College,
Delhi University

MY MOTHER BECAME a widow when I was eighteen years old. Today, she's been a widow far longer than the time she spent with Baba.

Initially, she was shell-shocked, but over the years, she evolved. Married when she had just about completed her matriculation exams, Baba, ten years older than her, was more than just a husband. She ruled his heart alright, but he mentored her about the ways of the world and the army life that she became part of since Baba was a doctor in the army. She was quite the ideal army wife managing home, hearth, four daughters and the immensely hectic social life within and outside the home.

Ma was always on her toes and engaged with something or the other that made her the queen of the household. Everyone knew Ma to be a very house-proud lady with an impeccable home. She prepared the most lavish of all spreads from scratch and was the perfect manager of her domestic space. Baba took care of decisions related to academics and career choices for the girls and Ma was only too happy about it.

When Baba passed away, she still had me in college and the third of us siblings preparing for the civil services examinations. Two daughters out of four yet to be settled. And Ma was not even fifty. Expectedly, she came apart and wanted to become a recluse, cut off all her hair and wear white. That is what she knew widows did. We did not let that happen. She busied herself with acts of domesticity which is what she had done all those earlier years. Now, she also looked after the grandchildren and went to whichever of the siblings needed her.

In the meantime, the third of the siblings, who was in the Indian Audit and Accounts Service, was posted to Calcutta and Ma went there to be with her and to finally move into the home that Baba had built for a retired life which he unfortunately never got to see. It is here that she came into her own. She started working voluntarily, thrice a week as a member of the All India Women's Conference where her task was to put labels on condiment packets prepared by the young girls being trained by the group.

This group of ladies who managed the local office became her new family and she began a new social life, often doing crazy things with them like watching two films in the movie hall on the same day, one after the other, apart from going for picnics and fairs or visiting temples and attending spiritual discourses. While Baba had been alive, she had never had time to be part of Durga Puja Committees, but now she became actively involved with them and would often reach the pandal in the wee hours of the morning to chop fruits and vegetables and later help to first set-up, then manage the food stalls. She would travel to us sisters, too, but was always eager to return to Calcutta, to her friends and, of course, her home which she reconstructed, several times, all on her own and managed all the payments of bills and utilities, with no help from any of us at all.

Ma is now 88. Independent in spirit still and resistant to the idea of staying permanently with her daughter, she chooses to continue to live by herself. Given her age, she is active and keeps herself as busy as she can. Many from her charmed circle of friends have left the world or the city and she misses them sorely.

AIWC activities which were affected during the Covid 19 pandemic have not picked up the pace they once had and besides Ma misses the older crowd she would chat with during those evenings. It is the evenings that she finds most difficult. The time passes slowly as there is no companion beside her. Her widowhood, almost forgotten by us over the passage of time as she was never free, once again hangs heavily over her head. She is well off, more than she was when she was married, and her health is obviously a matter of concern though she does keep herself fit. But there is inescapable loneliness. With it comes despondency and boredom. She laments that she has nothing left now and waits for the end.

In 2020, my second sibling, a retired eye specialist from the Armed Forces, lost her husband to the deadly Covid 19 virus. It was a bolt from the blue as my brother-in-law was the most fitness-conscious person in the family, and in his lifetime, the fittest too. But the virus was ruthless as we all know. My sister who had just about started enjoying her retired life with her husband after years of army life where the two were often separated due to different postings or due to war, suddenly found herself all alone in this huge penthouse lovingly made by her husband. With her son away at Singapore, she wondered how she would carry on. She works at an eye hospital five days a week, researches, teaches, publishes and keeps herself academically engaged. She now has a granddaughter whom she is only too happy to visit as often as possible. She looks after her ailing mother-in-law who lives in another state and needs constant care due to dementia. And she has turned to her abiding faith in God, seeking healing from grief through Krishna and religious sermons. She is extremely comfortably off and being a doctor, is able to look after her physical health, too. However, it is the mental health that suffers as she too misses deeply, her husband's companionship, a man who pretty much made all the decisions of the house, something she had always preferred. Now she has to decide for herself and turns often to her son to help her out. But it is not the same.

There is a reason why I have written about my mother and my sister in this afterword. Both are widows, but there's an ocean of difference between them, such as professional qualifications, social life and even, changing perceptions of women and widowhood since the eighties and now. The two are not alike at all, yet are bound together by the thread of loss and grief, by the waking up to another day of absence and the lying awake to another night of emptiness. There are similar fears. There are similar worries. There are similar hopes too, perhaps.

Widows are all connected in their hopes, fears and worries. However, the narrations we have seen in this book, so keenly researched, prove that those widows who do not enjoy any kind of financial empowerment and are left in the lurch by their families and often forgotten by society, at large and the government, in particular, perhaps do not have the luxury of thinking too much about their fears and worries. They are busy—in the act of staying alive, with dignity. Thank heavens there are people and organisations who want to reach out and help them do so—may their tribe increase.

As an educational institution, we would be failing in giving a complete education to our students if we did not sensitise them to the needs of those whose voices are generally unheard and neglected. Widows are one such group. As we learn about them, we must learn too, to admire them for they live their lives of pain and in many instances, of penury, with a quiet acceptance of life and death. It reminds me of the lines from the *Bhagavad Gita*:

na jāyate mriyate vā kadāchin
nāyaṁ bhūtvā bhavitā vā na bhūyaḥ
ajo nityaḥ śhāśhvato 'yaṁ purāṇo
na hanyate hanyamāne śharīre

The soul is neither born, nor does it ever die; nor having once existed, does it ever cease to be. The soul is without birth, eternal, immortal, and ageless. It is not destroyed when the body is destroyed.

May they teach us this essential truth through the way they lead their lives.

Bio-Notes of Contributors

Swati Pal

Swati Pal, Professor and Principal, Janki Devi Memorial College, University of Delhi, is a Fulbright-Nehru fellowship scholar, a Charles Wallace scholar and the first Asian scholar to receive the John McGrath Theatre Studies Scholarship at Edinburgh University. Author of several books on theatre, creative and academic writing, her newspaper articles articulate her views on education. Her areas of research interest include performance studies and cultural history. She translates from Hindi to English and several of her translations have been published. She writes poetry and her poems have appeared in many anthologies; she also has two collections titled *In Absentia* and *Forever Yours* and a curated collection called *Living On.* She is the Vice Chair of the Association for Commonwealth Literature and Language Studies in India and has been the recipient of several national and international awards, both as a teacher as well as an administrator.

Meera Khanna

Meera Khanna is the Trustee and President of the Guild of Service, which is an NGO in consultative status with

ECOSOC, UN. She is the Co-Founder of Everywoman Treaty for Ending Violence against Women and Girls. She is also the core committee member and Director of SANWED (South Asian Network for Widows Empowered in Development). She is the Director of the Global Alliance: Last Woman First. She is also advisor to the War Widows Association and a Trustee at Navdanya. Khanna is a renowned writer and gender rights activist with an impressive range of causes that she has supported and committees that she has led.

Malashri Lal

Malashri Lal is a Vice President and Executive Committee Member of the Guild of Service. She retired as a Professor from the Department of English, Delhi University. Malashri Lal has held various prestigious academic and administrative positions including that of Dean of Colleges, and Director of the Women's Studies Centre at DU. She is currently a member of the English Advisory Board at the Sahitya Akademi. She has published twenty-four books and has a long association with gender studies and culture. She has been a senior consultant to the Ministry of Culture, a UGC nominee on committees and a jury member of several international book awards. Some of her publications include *The Law of the Threshold: Women Writers in Indian English, Tagore and the Feminine*, and the 'goddess trilogy' coedited with Namita Gokhale*: In Search of Sita, Finding Radha*, and *Treasures of Lakshmi*. The Kalinga fiction award was given to *Betrayed by Hope: A Play on the Life of Michael Madhusudan Dutt,* that she co-authored with Namita Gokhale. Malashri's poetry collection, *Mandalas of Time (*2023) has been translated into Hindi. Her recent publications include *The Whispering*

Mountains: Marvellous Folktales from the Himalayas (co-edited with Namita Gokhale). Malashri Lal is the Secretary General of the SANWED (SouthAsian Network for Widows Empowerment in Development) Secretariat based at the Guild of Service, New Delhi, and she assists women's empowerment initiatives, specially overseeing educational programmes in Rajasthan.

Anita Singh

Anita Singh is a Professor and Head of the Department of English at Banaras Hindu University. She received a Fulbright-Nehru Visiting Scholar Fellowship for the year 2013-2014 at the University of Virginia, USA. She was a Fellow at the Indian Institute of Advanced Study in Shimla, India (2018–2020). Her recent publications are *Staging Feminisms: Gender, Violence, and Performance* (Routledge, 2021) and the two edited volumes *Gender, Space, and Resistance: Women and Theatre in India*, (DK Print World, 2013) and *Evolution of Tradition, Interrogating Transformations in Traditional Folk Performing Arts*, (London: HP Hamilton Limited, 2022). She is the President of The Asian-African Association for Women, Gender and Sexuality (AAAWGS).

Namita Sethi

Namita Sethi is an Associate Professor at the Department of English, Janki Devi Memorial College, University of Delhi. Her publications include *In Search of Delhi*, (with Jitender Gill, Routledge 2023), an edition of *Gulliver's Travels* (Worldview, 2023) and *Re-Discovering Delhi* (Pinnacle, 2021, co-edited with Jitender Gill)). She has an abiding interest in gender studies and has published and lectured widely on women in literature and culture. She is currently Director, Centre for Gender Equity Studies at JDM College. She received her PhD from the University of Delhi. She was an Associate at the Indian Institute of advanced Studies, Shimla.

Vasiraju Rajyalaskshmi

Vasiraju Rajyalakshmi is a Professor at the Department of Sociology, Janki Devi Memorial College. She received her PhD from Jawaharlal Nehru University and has been a Post-Doctoral Fellow at ICSSR. Her publications include *Language and Ethnic Identity in India* (Uppal Publishing House, 2010) and *Society: An insight* (Jawahar Publishing House, 2011). She has published many articles and contributed e-content for MOOC as well as for studies for senior secondary grades. She is regular panellist at Rajya Sabha TV. She has led many research projects and is Co-Director of the Centre for Gender Equity Studies, JDM College. She has served as Consultant to the Delhi government in the Women's Empowerment Cell and conducts workshops on Gender sensitisation for Delhi Police.

Tarun Sharma

Tarun Sharma is an Assistant Professor in the Department of English at Janki Devi Memorial College, University of Delhi. He completed his M Phil in English from the University of Delhi. His areas of interest are Partition Studies, Twentieth Century Modern Urdu Poetry and Sindhi Literature.

Ruchika Bhatia

Ruchika Bhatia currently holds the position of Assistant Professor in the English department at Janki Devi Memorial College, University of Delhi. Her primary research interests include gender studies, issues of sexuality, and the examination of gendered identities represented within society. Additionally, she focuses on the theme of sexual dissidence and its relevance in comprehending modernist ideologies. She also possesses a postgraduate degree in Advertising and Public Relations from the Indian Institute of Mass Communications, New Delhi, and has two years of professional experience in the corporate sector as a Media Planner.

Ankan Dhar

Ankan Dhar is an Assistant Professor in the Department of English, Janki Devi Memorial College, University of Delhi. His publications and areas of interest are in Indian Classical Literature and Aesthetics, Nineteenth and Twentieth Century Literature and in Gender Studies.

Vandana Madan

Vandana Madan is an Associate Professor of Sociology at Janki Devi Memorial College, University of Delhi. Her areas of academic interest include Indian society and culture, Environmental issues and Gender. She has several publications and her edited book, *The Village in India,* published by OUP is on the Social Science syllabus of over 20 Indian and Foreign Universities. Her essay on the Indian Village is essential reading for UPSC aspirants who have chosen Sociology as a discipline. She has spoken at many national and international seminars and conferences over the past four decades on the issues of gender, education and environment. She works closely with NGOs on gender and environment-related issues.

JDMC Students Research Team

Student Photo Editor

Himanshi Chawla, an English literature graduate from Janki Devi Memorial College. She is a published documentary photographer, with over four years of experience in photography and visual storytelling. Her work has been featured in cultural and heritage-focused books, with additional recognition from Photo Vogue for her fashion photography. Alongside her photography ventures, she builds photo albums, develops film scripts, and has experience in graphic design, marketing strategy, and has led a photography workshop at Delhi University.

RESEARCH TEAM MEMBERS

Research
Team Members

- Smriti Ahuja
- Aditi Chandra
- Himanshi Chawla
- Muskan Dhankher
- Muskaan Jain
- Arshpreet Kaur
- Priya Khandelwal
- Himanshi Khanna
- Sejal Khanna
- Mansi
- Sakshi Mishra
- Ayushi Pal
- Samriddhi Pendharkar
- Sucheta Raj
- Megha Saini
- Anchal Sethi
- Ishiqa Shadija
- Akshita Sharma
- Diksha Sharma
- Sakshi Sharma
- Harshita Singh
- U Sai Sruti
- Nikita Yadav
- Prerna
- Nitakshi

End Notes

Poverty has a Widow's Face

https://www.livemint.com/Politics/RjAdjOgWkNMqHGI1DqX8tJ/Census-reveals-gloomy-picture-of-life-in-femaleheaded-house.html

Government Initiatives on Basic Needs of Widows

- pib.gov.in
- www.wikipedia.org
- Indianlawportal.co.in
- A video on Bhajan Ashrams by Sulabh International TV

Widows in Recent Indian Fiction

- Basu, Bani. *Swet Patharer Thala.*1990. Translated from Bangla into
- English by Nandini Guha. *A Plate of White Marble.* New Delhi: Niyogi, 2020.Print.
- Brinks, Ellen. Anglophone Indian women writers, 1870-1920. VT: *Ashgate*, 2013. Print.
- Buitenen, Van ed. and translated. *The Mahabharata* (by Vyasa). I. The Book *of the Beginning.* Chicago U P, 1973. Print.
- Chakraborty, Aishika. *Widows of Colonial Bengal: Gender, Morality and Cultural Representation.* Delhi: Primus, 2023. Print.
- Chakravarti, Aruna. *The Inheritors.* New Delhi: Penguin, 2004. Print.

- *The Mendicant Prince*. New Delhi: Picador, 2022.Print.
- *Through a Looking Glass*: Stories. N Delhi: Om Books, 2022. Print.
- Khanna, Vikas. *The Last Color*. Delhi: Bloomsbury, 2018. Print.
- Roye, Susmita. *Mothering India: Women's Fiction in English Shaping Cultural History (1890-1947)*. N Delhi: OUP, 2020. Print.
- Sethi, Namita, 'A Compelling Mirror', Book Review of *Through the Looking Glass*: Stories by Aruna Chakravarti. Noida/Delhi: Om Books, 2022. *The Book Review*, Volume XLVII, no. 5, May 2023. Print.
- Sogani, Rajul. *The Hindu Widow in Indian Literature*. N Delhi: OUP, 2002. Print.

Sarat Chandra Chattopadhyay

Ambivalences in Representation

1. *Kulinism* or *kulin pratha* was introduced by King Ballala Sena (12th century CE), by which certain families of the upper three *varnas* were recognised as noble/superior. Males of such families were considered highly eligible, and often had multiple wives. This also led to a high number of widows.
2. In *Srikanta* (Book II, Ch. 15), Srikanta addresses Rajlakshmi as Rohini.
3. Brahmacharya is a concept in Hinduism, Buddhism, Jainism and Yoga. Originally formulated as a metaphysical practice it referred to a spiritual existence. More commonly it refers to an ascetic lifestyle involving sexual abstinence, vegetarianism and simple existence.
4. The concept of *parakiya prema* in Indian aesthetics can be compared to the courtly love tradition in medieval Europe.
5. In Indian aesthetics, *prema* and *kama* are expressions of the binary of spiritual and secular love. The former symbolises platonic devotion whereas the latter represents physical desire.
6. This corresponds very closely to the portrayal of Binodini's relationship with Bihari Babu in *Chokher* Bali.

7. Interestingly, another novel where Chattopadhyay moves beyond the institution of remarriage for his widow-characters is *Shubhada*. Lalana and Surendranath do not marry, but live together in a fulfilling relationship. It was written in 1898, but fearing an adverse response from the public, Chattopadhyay did not publish it. It was published posthumously in 1938.

- Bandyopadhyay, Asit Kumar. *History of Modern Bengali Literature.* Modern Book Agency Pvt. Ltd, 1986.
- Chattopadhyaya, Sarat Chandra. *Srikanta.* Translated by Aruna Chakravarti. Penguin Books India Pvt. Ltd., 1993.
- *The Final Question.* Translated by Members of the Department of English, Jadavpur University. Penguin Books India Pvt. Ltd, 2010.
- Chauhan, Vibha S. 'On the Becoming and Existence of Home: Inequities, Disparities and the Novel in India.' *Interpreting Homes in South Asian Literature.* edited by Malashri Lal and Sukrita Paul Kumar. Pearson Education, 2007.
- Chowdhury, Indira. 'Constructing Chastity: The Sati and the Widow in Nineteenth-Century Bengal.' *Women in History*, edited by Anuradha Chanda, et al., Jadavpur University, 2003.
- Kaviraj, Sudipta. *The Invention of Private Life: Literature and Ideas.* Columbia UP, 2015.
- Kumar, Radha. *The History of Doing: An Illustrated Account of Movements for Women's Rights and Feminism in India, 1800-1990,* Zubaan Publishers Pvt. Ltd., 2015.
- Mukherjee, Meenakshi. *Realism and Reality: The Novel and Society in India.* OUP, 1985.
- Roye, Susmita. *Mothering India: Women's Fiction in English Shaping Cultural History (1890-1947).* OUP, 2020.
- Sogani, Rajul. *The Hindu Widow in Indian Literature.* OUP, 2002.

Representation of Widows in Indian Advertising

- https://www.scirp.org/journal/paperinformation.aspx?paperid=108452
- https://journals.sagepub.com/doi/10.1177/037698360303000221
- https://devdutt.com/articles/advertising-widows/
- https://www.huffpost.com/entry/india-second-marriage-ad_n_4181192
- https://www.timeslive.co.za/sunday-times/lifestyle/2013-11-01-jewellery-advert-with-widow-remarrying-turns-heads-in-india/
- https://www.businessinsider.in/5-ads-that-defy-social-taboos-in-india/articleshow/47640779.cms
- https://www.exchange4media.com/advertising-news/tanishq-breaks-old-normscelebrates-the-beauty-of-remarriage-53273.html#:~:text=The%20ad%20beautifully%20breaks%20norms,on%20such%20a%20sensitive%20issue.
- https://brandkare.com/tanishq-wedding-film/
- https://www.youtube.com/watch?v=0WQcEbLE7SA
- https://www.youtube.com/watch?v=EqcNHhsNzeA
- https://www.youtube.com/watch?v=jqggcpL79qw

A Sociological Understanding of Widowhood in India

1. Gowda, Gomathi. (2021). *Mangalsutra: The sacred pendant of women as symbol of Marriage in India,* 6. 22-34.
2. Bhula Pooja (2013): *Dowry reversal in Assamese Culture*; www.dnaindia.com, accessed on 24-Jan-2022
3. *Women 2000: Widowhood: invisible women, secluded or excluded* Publication year: 2001
4. Census of India 2011, National Population Register & Socio Economic and Caste Census
5. *Widowhood in the Indian Society,* Radhika Kapur, March 2018

6. Pandey, Jatin & Gupta, Manish. (2019). *Religion in the Lives of Hindu Widows: Narratives from Vrindavan, India. Psychology of Religion and Spirituality.* 11. 91-100. 10.1037/rel0000230.
7. Hooda, Bhumika. (2022). *Analysing Modern day Witch Hunts in Rural India.* SSRN Electronic Journal. 10.2139/ssrn.4004027.
   - Bremmer, Jan, and Lourens Van Den Bosch, eds. *Between Poverty and the Pyre: Moments in the history of widowhood.* Routledge, 2002.
   - Chandrasekhar, C. & Ghosh, Jayati. (2017). *Widowhood in India.*
   - Chen, Martha Alter. Perpetual Mourning: *Widowhood in Rural India.* Oxford University Press, USA, 2001.
   - Dutt, Vijay, and Risto F Harma. *Invisible Forgotten Sufferers: The Plight of Widows Around the World.* Konark Publishers, 2010.
   - Hooda, Bhumika. (2022). *Analysing Modern Day Witch Hunts in Rural India.* SSRN Electronic Journal. 10.2139/ssrn.4004027.
   - https://censusindia.gov.in/vital_statistics/SRS_Report.
   - *Widows in India: Invisible Women Facing Invisible Problems* Joe Thomas — June 23, 2021.
   - *Widowhood: The Problems and Challenges Faced by Widows In India,* Rajal Dave, *International Journal of Advanced Research in Commerce, Management & Social Science* (IJARCMSS) 34 ISSN: 2581-7930, Impact Factor: 5.260, Volume 03, No. 04, October - December 2020, pp 34-36.
   - *Women 2000: Widowhood: Invisible Women, Secluded or Excluded.* HeadQuarters. N.p., n.d. Web. 30 Nov. 2014.

Sanyasa and Bhakti

The Widows of Vrindavan

- Census of India, censusindia.gov.in/census.website/
- Dubois .J.A (1959/1906). *Hindu Manners Customs and Ceremonies.* Oxford: The Clarendon Press.

- Dumont. L. (1980). *Homo Hierarchicus: The Caste system and its implications.* Chicago: The University of Chicago Press.
- Kinsley (1977). *The Death that Conquers Death: Dying to the World in Medieval Hinduism. In Religious Encounters with Death: Insights from the History and Anthropology of Religions* (eds) F Reynolds and E.H. Waugh. University Park and London: Pennsylvania State University Press. pp.97-108.
- Pearson, A. (1996). *Because it gives me Peace of Mind: Ritual Fasts in the Religious lives of Hindu Women.* New York: SUNY Press.

Meeting Mas at Parikrama Marg and Bhajan Ashrams

- Bhattacharya, Malini, *The Hidden Violence of Faith: The Widows of Vrindaban. Social Scientist.* Vol. 29, No. 1/2 (Jan. - Feb. 2001), pp. 75-83.
- Bhowmick, Nilanjana, *If You're an Indian Widow, Your Children Could Kick You Out and Take Everything TIME,* 2013.

Community as Home

Tale of Harmony among Hardships

1. *Dimensions of Deprivation*, a report on the poverty levels of Widows of Vrindavan. A survey by the Guild of Service. Supported by UNIFEM, published in 2010.
2. The quotation, 'To live is to suffer, to survive is to find some meaning in the suffering,' is from Friedrich Nietzsche's book titled *Twilight of the Idols*, specifically from a section called 'The Problem of Socrates.

Representation of Widows in Indian Cinema

1. Pande, Rekha. '*The Forgotten Widows of Vrindavan in India*', *Religion and Theology: Breakthroughs in Research and Practice.* IGI Global:2020. Pp 61-77.

2. Giri Mohini, *The Ongoing Tragedy of India's Widows, Women Under Siege*. Web. The ongoing tragedy of India's widows — Women's Media Center (womensmediacenter.com)
3. Kaur, Kanwaljit. *The Feminist Study of Widowhood In Women Centric Films of Hindi Cinema, JETIR* 2018, Volume 5, Issue 6.
4. Films and OTT:
   - Mehta, Deepa, '*Water*', Eagle Home Entertainment Pvt Ltd. 2005
   - '*Made in Heaven*', Amazon Prime 2019
   - Bist, Umesh, '*Pagglait*', Netflix 2021.
5. Survey Form:
   - Samriddhi Pendharkar, Priya K. (Janki Devi Memorial College)- Google Form Survey (Data collected and compiled)

JDMC Students' Research Team